WONDER

WONDER

AMAZING HOW A LITTLE WONDER CAN CHANGE THE WORLD

Lee Ihn (Ike)

ISBN: 1547203331
ISBN 13: 9781547203338

Dedicated to my family and friends
who have supported me, inspired me, and believed in me.

CONTENTS

ACKNOWLEDGEMENTS

I am very grateful to the many people who have supported me, inspired me, and believed in me throughout my life. This book is a retelling of my life experiences and central to these experiences are the many people whom I met and who helped me on my life journey. I would be nothing today without their constant attention, kindness, and advice, from which I benefitted tremendously. To them, I am eternally grateful.

> *"I am a part of all that I have met;*
> *Yet all experience is an arch wherethro'*
> *Gleams that untravell'd world whose margin fades*
> *For ever and forever when I move."*
> Alfred Lord Tennyson "Ulysses"

FOREWORD

Leaders often think they already know what their customers want. That is a huge mistake. There is always more room to learn. So how can we avoid the trap of our assumptions? If you've just asked yourself this question with me, you have already begun. That is the power of wonder.

Self-reflection in the quietness of one's own mind is not the habit of the ascetic who shuns society. Most great leaders in history develop a practice of setting time aside to meditate on their lot and the situation around them. To pause from daily life, to ask oneself questions, to think deeply of problems, to carefully arrive at solutions is key to leading effectively.

This book is a collection of ideas and lessons that I have come to believe after a life-long habit of looking at things around me with a critical eye, of constantly asking questions, and of always wondering. I hope you will find these musings as valuable to your own endeavors as they have been for me; and that you too will develop an enduring habit of self-reflection and wonder.

CHAPTER 1

WHY DO COMPANIES DIE?

*"To understand a man, you must first
walk a mile in his moccasin."*
NORTH AMERICAN INDIAN PROVERB

"I am dying, Egypt, dying."
ANTONY AND CLEOPATRA (IV, XV, 41)

*"The lessons I learned from the dark days at Alibaba
are that you've got to make your team have value,
innovation, and vision. Also, if you don't give up, you
still have a chance. And, when you are small, you have to
be very focused and rely on your brain, not your strength."*
JACK MA

F OR MORE THAN TWENTY YEARS, I have been reviewing fifty to one hundred business pitches each month. I've had the opportunity to invest in scores of projects through my incubation center I ran at the Stanford Research Park in the mid '90s and later through my own venture capital company. Some of these businesses have grown to be successes making hundreds of millions and achieving highly valued IPOs. And some turned out to be failures. I once invested in a businessman who had everything: a track record, the right team, a great network equipment product. And I not only lost my money, I watched a similar business I had passed on become a huge hit. Why would a promising idea led by a person with the right background fall apart?

I have also worked for several decades as a management consultant for companies in the IT, telecommunications, and defense electronics sectors that were once successful but began to struggle with declining revenue. What were they doing wrong?

A popular dictum in the entrepreneur world is that nine out of ten start-ups fail. In 2003, Paul Graham, founder of Silicon Valley's most famous incubator Y-Combinator, tweeted that thirty-seven of his over five hundred companies at the time were worth $40 million or more. That is already a low percentage of success—but when we adjust for the fact that Y-Combinator accepts only three to five percent of applicants into its program, we note that these five hundred companies were likely selected from 10,000 applicants. In other words, out of thousands of start-ups pitched to Y-Combinator, only a handful grew to be worth several million dollars or have a successful exit.

In 2012, the Ewing Marion Kauffman Foundation published their report on the venture capital market and reported that only twenty of one hundred venture funds generated returns that beat a public-market equivalent by more than three percent annually. The majority of funds—sixty-two out of one hundred—failed to exceed returns available from the public markets. Since venture funds represent the diversified risks of their portfolio, companies comprising these portfolios have a very low survivability rate indeed.

What about large, well established companies? Do they endure forever? History is littered with the carcasses of once-great conglomerates. Montgomery Ward, Pan-Am, and Enron were once icons of American ingenuity and do not exist today. RCA, TWA, and MCI, acronyms that were once commonplace, have altogether dropped from our lexicon. But, what is more puzzling is that many large companies fail when their market factors are at their best.

Let us take the example of Eastman Kodak, the venerable American company established in 1888 by a genius founder, George Eastman. Mr. Eastman invented the roll film, which allowed his company to sell cameras cheap and the film at above-market profit margins. The roll film was also the basis for the motion picture film and subsequent movie industry. Kodak's contribution in making both picture taking and movie making mainstays of modern life is likely unmatched by any other company. At its peak in the late 1970s, Kodak commanded ninety percent of the film market and eight-five percent of the camera market in the USA. Its influence was so strong words like "Kodak moment" were commonly used to mean a beautiful picture-perfect moment worth capturing.

However, it all changed in the 1990s. The company missed the transition to digital photography despite having invented and patented much of the technology. Facing stiff competition, especially from aggressive Japanese companies, Kodak's revenue plummeted. It tried several new strategies, changed multiple executives, laid off thousands of employees, but in vain. In 2012, the company declared bankruptcy and filed for Chapter 11 protection. This all happened at a time when capturing, recording, analyzing, editing, storing and sharing of pictures exploded. In 2011 alone, 380 billion photos were taken. Why did Kodak fail when the market it literally created was at its peak?

Is death inevitable for businesses?

Why is it so difficult for businesses to take off? And, even if they take off, why is it so difficult for businesses to stay alive? Death is life's most certain predicament. We all die. As we age, our muscles debilitate, our senses attenuate, our memories faint, our mind deteriorates until our whole body succumbs. Death for all of us is the most natural of all endings. Beyond the organic, all objects around us expire too. Houses crumble, bridges collapse, cars rust, roads crack, and junk gets scrapped. And when it comes to the intangibles, even ideas, the most everlasting of our mind's accomplishments, get superseded, replaced, and altered.

It is easy to understand and to readily accept that life, objects, and ideas would have expiration dates. The question then is: can we ever design entities to be everlasting, or in the practical sense, entities that last for a very long time beyond the expiration dates of life, objects, and ideas? Theoretically, an entity comprised of ever changing or evolving life could last forever. The entity would replace the expiring component by a new fresh substitute, maybe better component, and avoid the demise trap. What are such entities? Universities, governments, and businesses are all entities that are made up of life, objects, and ideas and that could theoretically last forever if they are regularly refreshed.

Many universities have lasted for centuries and are still going strong—the oldest university in the world is the University of al-Qarawiyyin, founded in 859 AD in Fez, Morocco. The University of Bologna, Italy, was founded in 1088 AD and is the oldest in Europe. Al-Azhar University in Cairo was founded in 970 AD and the University of Cambridge was founded in 1209 AD. All these institutions have survived for centuries and are likely to be in operation for many centuries to come.

A government system can last for a very long time if it is not built around one person, and regularly updates its infrastructure, and has room to allow its ideas to be amended, and implements some structure of checks and balances across its branches. A government lacking these properties is fragile and a government with such flexibility is, to borrow Nassim Taleb's term, anti-fragile. Liberal democracies that embody systems that are regularly refreshed through popular vote are among the most stable governance structures in human history.

Similarly, well-run businesses could theoretically last in perpetuum. The businesses would replace their management and personnel when their performances falter to maintain their energy and vitality; would replace machines and equipment when they fail; and would replace their ideas and products when they stop selling. However, whereas institutions like universities and popularly elected government like liberal democracies have lasted for a very long time, outliving their founders by centuries, very few businesses can claim such durability.

In fact, businesses are among the hardest of entities to keep alive. Not only do businesses expire all the time, most new businesses fail to even get off the ground. Many businesses fail when the factors that enable them are at their most propitious. This is truly dumbfounding because we apply the most efficient operations, the largest amount of money, and the best brains to run businesses and to keep them alive. Why then are businesses a prominent exception among such entities?

The Hindustan Ambassador

The industrialist and billionaire Indian family, the Birlas, opened one of India's first automobile manufacturing companies, Hindustan Motors, in 1942 shortly before India's independence. The company produced their cars based on the British Morris Oxford models—Morris Oxfords themselves having been in operation in the United Kingdom since 1913. In 1957, Hindustan Motors reintroduced the car to Indian roads in 1958 as the Hindustan

Ambassador. The company would go on to produce the same car for over four decades. During those years, they hardly ever paid attention to their customers' needs and rarely innovated on the design or features of the car.

The Ambassador was the very definition of car in India. It was in turn a symbol of status for the rich, the ultimate gift from the bride family to the groom at many Indian weddings, an emblem of patriotism for the politician, a trait of resilience on the poorly maintained Indian roads, a livelihood for the thousands of car mechanics trained in its repair, and a deity to many taxi drivers carting millions of passengers in bustling Indian cities. In 1996, there were 33,000 Ambassador taxis in Calcutta alone! Yearly, on the Vishwakarma Puja festival taxi drivers would decorate and literally worship the cars in the name of Vishwakarma, the Hindu god and divine architect.

What the Ambassador was not was a customer's dream vehicle. The car was not designed to be sleek; it was, in fact, bulky, with a comically high ceiling. Hormazd Sorabjee, the editor of Autocar India, best described the challenges the Ambassador posed to its customers in an article titled "An epitaph for India's 'appalling' national car." Here are excerpts from that article: "You needed really strong triceps to work the ridiculously heavy steering, the deftness of a surgeon to slot home the spindly column shifter into each gear (shifting from second to third gear was an art form) and immense strength to make the car stop—you had to nearly stand on the brakes. And the handbrake? It rarely worked but instead spawned a generation of drivers that could easily do hill starts deftly balancing the accelerator and brake. And there were Ambassador jokes aplenty, my favourite one being: "The only thing that doesn't make a sound in an Ambassador is the horn!""

And yet despite all these issues, the Ambassador sold aplenty for almost forty years—during a time when the Indian government severely limited production of domestic cars and controlled import of foreign cars. Hindustan Motors controlled 70% of the Indian car market even when it was not uncommon for the company to take one year to fulfill a car order.

All that changed very suddenly when the government liberalized the economy and encouraged innovation. Customers fled the Ambassador at lightning speed as soon as they had a better alternative. The affection for the Ambassador turned to scorn. Diehard fans were nostalgic but never wasted one minute going for a better car from the competition. The Ambassador had been the official car of the Prime Minster of India since the country's independence. But, in 2005 the Prime Minister, Mr. Atal Bihari Vajpayee, got stuck in his Ambassador when, for some unknown reasons, both the rear doors got jammed. The Prime Minister, who was well in his eighties, had to crawl over the front seats and over the gear lever to get out. By evening, the official car was replaced by a brand new BMW!

The shifting landscape

Consider this: for 10,000 years until the 1700s humanity largely depended on agriculture as its primary mode of survival. Scholars call this time the Agricultural Age. Starting in the 1700s, humans

WHY DO COMPANIES DIE?

invented a number of machines that would change their destiny—the cotton gin, the steam engine, the light bulb, and so on that would usher humanity into the Industrial Age. That period would last for 250 years. Towards the end of the twentieth century, William Shockley invented the transistor that heralded the Information Age. That last age would see the advent of the computer, the mobile phone, and the internet among other electronic devices that radically improved our standard of living as measured by practically all metrics—from survival rate after childbirth to life expectancy. Are we still living in the Information Age? Futurist David Houle argues that we have already transitioned into a Fourth age—the Shift Age!

According to Houle, we are currently in an era of transformation, experiencing three forces defining this new age: the world has become more of a village, the individual has become more empowered, and there has been an explosive growth in technological connectedness.

Aided by efficient and low cost travel technologies, the world indeed has turned into a big village in the years since World War II. There is no area left on Earth that has not been explored or that is now unreachable. Goods, services, and ideas now flow freely across borders. This has resulted in a convergence of universal ideas—from basic concepts of freedom to economic models and political structures. The numbers of democratically elected governments, as an example, doubled between 1975 and 2005. Similarly, many countries liberalized their economies towards a more market-driven, liberal, and capitalistic system. The fate of the Ambassador as described above was doomed when India liberalized its economy and opened up its market to foreign car companies. China's liberalization of its economy catapulted the country forward but also closer to the West. Cultures and traditions are blending. Teenagers in New York, London, Seoul, Rio, and Cairo all dress the same today and often times enjoy the same types of music. Accordingly, expectations and desires are converging.

Similarly, over the past years the world has seen development of various rights that have empowered the individual. These rights range from women's rights to minority rights to children's rights to alternative lifestyle rights. There is now a general belief in many countries that these rights are basic human rights that ought to be given to the individual solely by virtue of birth. The laws and social mores of many countries are being challenged and upgraded to guarantee these rights. Conversely, there has been a weakening of traditional power structures—be they government, large corporations, or even socio-religious bodies. This shift has empowered individuals in deciding their fate, their needs and how those needs are to be fulfilled.

Regarding technology connectedness, in just ten years we are more connected as a species than ever. The World Wide Web is already speeding towards its fourth revision—starting with basic communication such as email and FTP (Web 1.0), moving to database structures and HTML (Web 2.0), then on to the semantic web with wikis and social media (Web 3.0), to the intelligent web with distributed search and personal agents (Web 4.0). These technologies have fueled products that have made distances irrelevant, have brought humanity closer together, and are changing our behaviors. Consider this: as of 2014, there were 1.32 billion users on Facebook, over one billion users uploading one hundred hours of video on YouTube per minute, 284 million Twitter users sending 500 million tweets per day, 332 million users on LinkedIn, 200 million users on Instagram uploading sixty million photos per day, 209 million blogs on Tumblr, 70 million users on Pinterest, and 300 million users of Skype. In February 2016, the number of monthly users of WhatsApp crossed the one billion mark! Never in the history of humanity has information been democratized so dramatically.

These forces have empowered the individual customer like never before. They have given the customer the power, the access, and the tools to demand products and services as they want them. In such an age, the old manufacturer-to-customer model, like the Hindustan Motors' Ambassador car, is doomed to fail. The wise business executive should be savvy enough to bring the customer into the center of the design and innovation process and to serve customers a product and service just as they want it.

Customer feedback is your lifeline

In an era where customer has massive amount of information available at their fingertips, the task of putting a product up for sale can be daunting. A bad review gone viral may be sufficient to kill the product before it even launches. A two out of five-star rating on a service, whether it be waiting on a customer at a restaurant or streaming a movie over the Internet, is sufficient to drive sales away. A picture or a video capturing poor working conditions at a far-flung plant can doom your brand. Indeed, we have come a long way from Henry Ford's days when he said, "Any customer can have a car painted any color that he wants so long as it is black."

Should a company then fear this new power vested in the customer? Should a company be paralyzed and take a thousand precautions on how it messages and markets its products to a vocal mass? Is the Shift Age going to stifle innovation?

On the contrary, the Shift Age is a unique opportunity for businesses to stay alive by optimizing their products for their customers and staying relevant in a quickly changing market. Never before has information and intelligence about customer needs become more freely and more widely available. Smart businesses would never shy away from such a gold mine of data but rather would embrace the data and co-opt the customers in ideating, innovating, conceptualizing, designing, manufacturing, marketing, and selling the products. The customer can now be leveraged at every instance in a product lifecycle.

Before you even conceptualize your next product, pay attention to where customers are having problems. Scan the blogs and social networks looking for pain points in the domain where your company operates. It is difficult to create a product and then convince a market of its benefits. It is much easier to identify a pain point and create a product to alleviate that pain. Once you have identified the pain points, participate in the online discussions, ask questions, test answers to further understand the true nature of the friction. Replace your pavement interviews with analytical tools that can mine this data for customer insight. Let the crowd be your R&D center!

Then use the customer at large to test ideas. Focus groups are very much a relic of the past where a very small sample of a market segment provides often-biased feedback on your company ideas. In today's Shift Age of social technologies, test ideas early and often. Do not wait for the ideas to be finalized before launching the product. Rather build, improve, and iterate quickly. Software companies have learned to do that effectively. Companies like Google often release software continuously in beta versions, co-opting the customer in short iterative cycles to test their releases.

Finally, learn to capitalize on the language of social media to market a product. Understand the psychology of crowds and how opinions or memes get started and and spread. Identify your early adopters and influencers and reward them for using your products. Co-opt the power of many to brag about your product. Leverage all the social media outlets. Let the customer be your marketer and your best salesman.

In the Shift Age, power has transferred from the manufacturer to the customers. The Hindustan Motors Ambassador model is dead. While appearing daunting, this new age is a boon for smart companies who can capitalize on the power of the customer to continually reinvent their company and stay relevant to the customer long into the future.

CHAPTER 2

WHAT IS WRONG WITH AIRLINERS?

"Look beneath the surface let not the several quality of a thing nor its worth escape thee."
MARCUS AURELIUS ANTONIUS

"The ultimate measure of a man is not where he stands in moments of comfort and convenience, but where he stands at times of challenge and controversy."
MARTIN LUTHER KING, JR.

"It is in your moments of decision that your destiny is shaped."
TONY ROBBINS, LIFE COACH AND SELF-HELP AUTHOR

I TRAVEL ABOUT EIGHT TIMES PER year between Asia and the United States so I spend a great deal of time in airports, airplanes, hotels, and restaurants. Some fine restaurants and hotels have won my loyalty and keep me coming back time and again by thinking of the smallest details that make my visit enjoyable.

One of my favorite places to eat is a famous steak restaurant in New York. It can take seven months to get a table but from greeting to goodbye they are giving special service designed thoughtfully for me and each member of my party. The temperature is right, the lighting is right, their staff use gracious language and immediately fix any mistakes. The servers watch before they interrupt with a question or a plate. This is important, because I can't have a business negotiation in a restaurant that distracts from our dialogue.

I've also had too many experiences at restaurants where my party and I had to deal with the server instead of the server dealing with us. And some of these terrible experiences might surprise you. I'll never forget a dinner I had in a pricey new Asian restaurant with a celebrity chef that opened to much fanfare in Los Angeles. A good friend and I waited in a long line for our table, and the food was good. But the service was slow and the servers were rude and lacked training. I mentioned my food was a little salty and our server actually said, "That is what the dish is supposed to taste like."

When a customer says the food is salty, it is salty! I made a bet on how far that restaurant will go with my friend. He said six months and I said eight months. We were both wrong. Two months later that restaurant closed.

I think all companies can learn valuable lessons from the service sector. Who is the most important person in the restaurant? The celebrity chef? Who is the most important person on a plane? The pilot? A VIP guest? Who is the most important person in a company? The CEO?

Any company with a culture that only the supports the happiness of a CEO or executive will result in endless issues. Delta Airlines has instituted a brilliant profit-sharing model with its employees to encourage personal investment in the company's success from each staff member. Instead of all employees working for the top one percent, all employees work for themselves. Unfortunately, not all airlines follow this practice.

Nutrage

It was a relatively pleasant winter day at New York's John Fitzgerald Kennedy International Airport on the fifth of December 2014. The temperature hovered around forty degrees Fahrenheit and there was not an inch of snow on the ground. The Korean Air flight KA 82 bound for Incheon was scheduled to depart and arrive on time. For an airline that has been consistently ranked as one of the top flight service providers in the world, on-time departure and arrival were of particular importance. The airline's motto was, after all, "Excellence in Flight" and it promised every customer an experience "Beyond Your Imagination." Over the years, Korean Air's efficiency, professionalism, and high quality service had become factors of pride not only for the airline employees but for the whole country of South Korea. The airline seems to be voicing the Korean people's aspirations to reach the sky.

Ms. Heather Cho is a charismatic forty-year-old. One could have safely bet that Ms. Cho was one of a handful of people destined to reinvent the meaning of hospitality. Equipped with degrees from Cornell University School of Hotel Administration with an MBA from the University of Southern California, she joined Korean Air in 1999 and quickly rose through the ranks to lead the Catering and In-flight Sales Business, as well as the Cabin and Hotel Service Business, for Korean Air. In those roles, Ms. Cho was the single most important person in the company responsible for customer experience. In addition, Ms. Cho served on the advisory board of Nayang Business School. Good fortune not only blessed Ms. Cho with brains and beauty, but also bestowed upon her impeccable lineage. Ms. Cho was born into a chaebol (family-controlled business conglomerate) and is the daughter of Cho Yang-ho, the chairman of Korean Air.

Ms. Cho caught flight KA 82 on December fifth traveling first class. Even though she was traveling in a personal capacity and not officially as an Executive Vice President of the airline, she must have felt proud as she took her seat in the first class cabin. Everything around her was a testament of what she had accomplished in a relatively short career. We will never know whether she had a rough day in New York or whether she was eager to return home to Seoul for some pressing matters, but Ms. Cho was not in the greatest of moods. As she sat down in the comfortable seat waiting for the airplane to push out to the runway, she surveyed the cabin experience and something bothered her. As the plane started taxying for takeoff, a junior flight attendant brought her a few Macadamia nuts and committed, in her mind, one of the gravest faux pas of first class service—he served her the nuts in a bag and not on a plate! The seemingly inconsequential detail of the mode of nut-serving by the flight attendant tripped Ms. Cho's mood from glum to rage. It was the nut that cracked the airline EVP's back! What followed would tarnish an executive, a family, and a company, triggering far-flung debates on whether Korea's custom of doing businesses through chaebols is anachronistic with modern times.

Ms. Cho shouted at the flight attendant, jabbed him with a document folder, demanded that he kneel down and apologize. Then she fired him on the spot. At that point, had she calmed down and composed herself, the episode would have only been another occasion of office politics gone too far and would have remained within the company. But, Ms. Cho was not satisfied. She commanded the pilot to turn the plane around, return to the terminal in order to expel the flight attendant from the plane. At that moment, the welfare of the 250 customers on board did not cross her mind. Not for a minute did she pause to ask herself what the impact of her request would have on those who paid to travel with the airline. Would they worry that something was wrong with the plane? Would they suffer poor service now that there would be one less flight attendant on board? Would they be late for a reunion with their own families? At that moment when she should have shown character and leadership, in this brief instance when she lost her temper, at that critical time the Greeks called kairos, Ms. Cho failed as an executive.

The plane finally reached Incheon eleven minutes late—not a terrible delay. But, soon questions were raised as to whether Ms. Cho overstepped her functions as an executive of the company. Did she feel invincible because she is the daughter of the chairman? Did she have the right to not only reprimand an employee but belittle him and fire him on the spot? Korean Air first issued a statement claiming that monitoring employees' performance was part of Ms. Cho's job responsibilities. However, the Transportation Ministry noted that she was traveling in her own personal capacity. After a few days of high drama and press commentaries, Ms. Cho dressed in black and with head bowed accepted all responsibility and made a tearful apology. Her dad, Korean Air's chairman, apologized as well taking the blame for "not raising his daughter well." With mounting criticisms, Ms. Cho resigned from the company. Then on Christmas day, less than twenty days after the incident, the Seoul Western District Court ordered her detained for violating the safety procedures of a Korean vessel.

Ms. Cho was charged with violating aviation safety law, obstructing justice, and assaulting a member of the cabin crew. Prosecutors demanded a three-year sentence. In February 2015, Ms. Cho was found guilty and given a twelve-month sentence and later released. The flight attendant further filed a civil lawsuit with the Supreme Court of the State of New York against both Ms. Cho and Korean Air. The case was subsequently remanded to the Korean Justice Department. It appears that the ordeal for both Ms. Cho and Korean Air is far from over. In the end, Ms. Cho's family has to spend way more time and effort to regain the respect of customers and employees due to this incident.

Snowstorm at Midway

Almost to the day, nine years before the Korean Air incident at JFK International Airport, Southwest Airlines Flight 1248 was scheduled to arrive at Chicago's Midway International Airport from the Baltimore-Washington International Airport. The weather on that December 8, 2005 was miserable, typical of dreary Chicago winter days. The Windy City was being visited by a snowstorm and eight inches of snow had already accumulated on the ground. The weather was cold, a heavy wind was blowing, and visibility was poor. The pilots of Flight 1248 could only see less than one mile ahead of them. With ninety-eight passengers on board, the Boeing 737 circled over a small area in northwest Indiana several times while the pilots decided what course of action they should take next.

At that critical moment, the pilots had an important decision to make. They had three choices: continue circling in the air waiting for the weather to improve, divert the plane to the nearby O'Hare International Airport, which has a longer and safer runway, and land there, or attempt landing at the planned destination, Midway itself. The first two options would delay the flight's onward journey, cause passengers to miss connecting flights, and be expensive for Southwest. With the runway at Midway cleared of snow, the pilots made a fateful call and decided to land the plane on Runway 13 Center. However, things went terribly wrong as soon as the airplane touched down. Given the weather, wind, speed, and weight of the aircraft, the plane needed more runway than the available length of Runway 13 Center. It was apparent that the plane was moving too fast, was too heavy, and the conditions were too unfavorable for it to safely come to a stop. To add to the issues, the cockpit crew deployed thrust reversers a few seconds late to slow the plane down. The plane skidded. The nose gear collapsed. The whole aircraft overshot the runway. And the plane crashed into a barrier wall surrounding the airport, colliding with multiple cars before coming to rest on Central Avenue outside of the airport.

The airplane hit at least three cars on that busy intersection. Six-year-old Joshua Woods was in a car with his parents and two siblings at that unfortunate moment in that unfortunate location. They were on their way from Leroy, Indiana, to visit Joshua's grandmother in Chicago. When the plane hit his car, Joshua was killed on the spot. His parents and one sibling were injured but were in fair condition. His infant brother was injured and was in serious condition. In addition, five occupants of the second car were critically injured and four occupants of the third car were seriously injured. Three passengers on the plane suffered minor injuries. In all, twelve persons were taken to the hospital. The incident was the first and only incident with a fatality in Southwest's forty-four-year history.

Now when such an incident happens, executives of the company involved usually take time to gather information and form an accurate opinion of what went wrong. They are hesitant to make public statements right away and are reluctant to comment on the situation, as the details are still murky. They neither accept blame right away nor blame others right away. Often times, the CEO remains silent and stays in the background and delegates the response to the media and PR team. After all, these are moments that can break a CEO's carefully crafted career and legacy. Showing too much empathy is akin to admitting liability.

But Southwest CEO Gary Kelly's reaction following this incident departed from the traditional and would set an example of how executives should actually behave to always put their customers first. Within three hours after the crash, CEO Kelly held a media press conference at Southwest's Dallas headquarters. He was open and transparent, and committed to doing everything possible to get to the bottom of the accident. He shared the company's and his personal condolences to the victims of the crash. Overnight, he sent a team of ninety-four members of the airline's Go Team, arriving at Chicago at 3:25AM, to assist with the National Transportation Safety Board investigation of the incident. Then early the following morning at 7:30 a.m., he again met with a few reporters at the headquarters to update the media and the public. After that meeting, he boarded a second special flight with more employees bound for Chicago. Once on the ground in Chicago, he called a press conference and began with the following words: "There are no words to adequately convey our grief and sorrow. . . The entire Southwest family is grieving this loss." Subsequently, Kelly travelled around the city and met with the victims and family members of the victims to express his personal condolences.

Commenting on Kelly's approach to crisis management and to staying laser-focused on their customers, Jonathan Bernstein, president of California-based Bernstein Crisis Management, said, "Southwest's safety record had been a major selling point, a unique proposition. And, its reputation for safety, quirky-friendly service and financial stability should help it move quickly past the tragedy in consumers' minds. Any company that creates a cushion of goodwill with all its stakeholders before a crisis occurs will survive a crisis better than a company that hasn't done that in advance. And nobody has done a better job of that in the country than Southwest." Pete Wentz, an Executive Vice President with the PR firm APCO Worldwide, said of Southwest and Kelly: "They stepped right in front, right away. Their CEO was right out front, right away. That's unique."

Organizations many times live or die based on how they react during times of crises. Southwest would go on to become a stronger company, one that customers still trust and love to this day. Gary Kelly was named one of the best CEOs in America in 2008, 2009, and 2010 by Institutional Investor magazine. Southwest share price on the New York Stock Exchange, under the leadership of CEO Kelly, appreciated by 400% from the day after the crash to the beginning of 2015. Meanwhile, disappointment and anger at Korean Air continue to mount and Chairman Cho Yang-ho's long-term prospects appear dicey at best. Koran Air stocks were still down 35% in the couple of years following the nutrage incident.

Not so friendly skies

The entire world saw the unforgettable video of Asian Dr. David Dao being dragged from his seat on a United Flight 3411 on April 13, 2017 by security officials because United oversold the flight and needed extra seats to get their flight crew to their next destination.

United struggled to find their public footing after the incident. At first CEO Oscar Munoz defended his employees, but after a swift and severe public backlash progressively, and tearfully, began apologizing and overhauling the airlines policies on overselling flights and related compensation. But that one moment of poor customer service is resulting in a direct loss of over one billion dollars for United. CEO Oscar Munoz is also losing his potential chairman seat. Time will tell if he is allowed to keep his job at all.

Many Asian people were already uncomfortable flying on American-based airlines. I wonder how many Asians will now forever avoid American transportation services. This one incident will likely have industry-changing impacts. Now we might think such a clear lesson in placing your customers first would be quickly learned and embraced by all companies. No one wants to be the next United. But service doesn't improve on a constant upward trajectory like technology often does. Service is impacted constantly by the people who touch it. It depends on your employees being constantly well-trained, and sometimes even on whether they have a bad day or a good day.

There are many lessons to be learnt from these airline examples. First, taking care of your customers is always important. But at times of crises, at times when information is scarce, at times when a lot is at stake, customer care is especially vital. Great generals are not defined in times of peace but rather in times of war. Similarly, great leaders are not defined in times of calm but rather in times of crises.

Consider this—Korean Airlines leadership's attempt to appease the passengers who witnessed the nutrage incident on flight KA 82 was to send them a miniature model Korean Airlines jetliner. What were they thinking? Did they really believe that a toy airplane would win the customers' loyalty and gain their favorable statements when interviewed by the press about the incident? This shows a complete failure of leadership, a complete lack of intellectual acumen dealing with a serious problem, and a complete corruption of judgment about the consequences of shallow decision-making.

United was also slow to understand the impact of their incident. The public quickly got the impression that United would only change the minimally required amount. Their competitors, including Delta, released new policies on overselling and dramatically increased their vouchers even before United did! Contrast this to the reaction of Southwest's CEO Kelly after the incident at Midway. He showed extreme care and extreme empathy, at large expenses to the company, for the customers impacted by the incident. He personally took ownership of the problem and led his team in tackling the issue at hand. In times of crises, the leader should abandon all attempts to rationalize or excuse the situations and should instead place the customers well-being first and foremost.

Second, companies should strive to redirect employees' loyalty away from the management/owner to customers. In many Asian companies, including Korean Air, employees live in a combination of fear and admiration for their bosses. They consciously and subconsciously elevate their bosses to near-king or near-queen status! It is common, for example, in such companies to have employees sit around and wait in the office after their work is done and only leave for home after the boss leaves. And, if the boss comes to the office on a Saturday or holiday, all the employees will be there too. Some of that stems from a culture of respect, but it also stems from a culture of attributing too much importance to hierarchies with scions of historical families, or chaebols, sitting on top. These bosses, in turn, favor those most loyal to them—so, pleasing the big boss, for example, is vital to promotions or guaranteeing tenure in the company. But, the boss is not the one who spends money to keep the company afloat—customers do. Switching focus away from the customer, who should really be the true boss, to the office boss is bound to result in problems sooner or later.

Southwest Airlines, on the other hand, is all about the customer. Their culture is one where the customer feels welcome and comfortable. Every aspect of the company is redirected to please the customer. Southwest's stock ticker, for example, is LUV. Its motto is FUN. Its employees are trained to treat customers as if they are part of their own family. Formal structures and hierarchies do not hold. Rather, every employee is encouraged to go to great lengths to get the customers to smile. The employee at the ticket counter will ask you about your day, the bag checker will be dressed informally, and the flight attendant will joke when reading the in-flight safety precautions. In an age where competition is stiff and customers have many options, focusing on customers and not on the office boss is the formula for success.

Third, companies should train their leaders to prepare for situations of crisis. Companies should put in place protocols of behavior, documented processes to follow, and response teams to react when crises occur. It is a given that in a complex world, things will not always work according to plans. Whether from natural disasters or man-made mistakes, companies will every now and then face very challenging situations. While there is no way to plan for the unknown, a culture that places the well-being of customers first provides a reference toolkit, a manual if you will, on how to respond and react in tough situations.

CHAPTER 3

WHAT MADE SUSHI AN INTERNATIONAL FOOD?

"Verba movent, exempla trahunt"
(Words move people, examples compel them)
LATIN PROVERB

*"Jiro Ono serves Edo-style traditional sushi, the same
20 or 30 pieces he's been making his whole life, and he's
still unsatisfied with the quality and every day wakes
up and trains to make the best. And that is as close to
a religious experience in food as one is likely to get."*
ANTHONY BOURDAIN, CHEF, AUTHOR AND CNN HOST

*"Always look ahead and above yourself. Always
try to improve on yourself. Always strive to elevate
your craft. That's what he taught me."*
YOSHIKAZU ONO, JIRO ONO'S ELDEST SON

S USHI RESTAURANTS ARE commonplace in most American cities today, but that was not always the case. I still remember when I started my career in Santa Monica, California, there was only one Sushi restaurant for miles. The restaurant served a very focused customer segment and mainly Asians. Today, in the same suburb, you can find a sushi restaurant at almost every strip mall. And these new age sushi restaurants serve everybody—from Generation Y high-schoolers in torn jeans to first generation immigrants working at the nearby Fortune 50 technology companies.

How is it that sushi, a foreign food consisting of raw fish, little seasoning, and served cold (a foreign food both in geography and composition) became such a popular food for so many people in the cities of America?

California roll

In the early 1960s, the president of Japan's Mutual Trading Company, Mr. Noritoshi Kanai, introduced an American business associate, Mr. Harry Wolff, to Edomae-sushi in Japan. Mr. Wolff was so impressed by the dish that when he came back to Los Angeles, he opened the Kawafuku Restaurant in "Little Tokyo" in Los Angeles. The restaurant served traditional Japanese food, like teriyaki and tempura, on the ground floor. But it hosted a sushi bar on the top floor. Sushi master Shigeo Saito was brought in from Japan to prepare the intricate delicacies. Along with his wife, who served as the only waitress, master Saito introduced sushi for the first time to a mix of Japanese and American patrons. His menu was an immediate hit and soon more restaurants were opening up and more chefs were flying in from Tokyo to prepare sushi in America.

In 1970, the first sushi bar outside of Little Tokyo, Osho, opened in Hollywood. Located in the heart of America's entertainment industry, the restaurant served celebrities, trendsetters, and risk-takers alike. These thrill-seekers tasted, tried, ate, and fell in love with sushi. They then raved about it on media channels to which they had ample access. This gave sushi exposure and aided its popular growth.

Then, sometime in the 1970s, a sushi chef named Ichiro Mashita at the Tokyo Kaikan restaurant, also in Los Angeles, faced a challenge. Tuna, used in maki roll, is a seasonal fish and not always available. The chef needed consistency to serve a clientele year-round. He could not make sushi throughout the year if the main ingredients were only available for part of the year. So he looked for an ingredient that could replace the tuna and yet provide the same mouth feel and the luscious texture of the fish. He decided to substitute the tuna with avocado—a never before tried experiment! He added crabmeat to substitute for the now missing tuna fish flavor. That experimentation with sushi went against centuries of traditional Japanese traditions.

However, there was still something in Mr. Mashita's invention that was putting some of his clients off. Initially, the roll was served traditionally with a crisped seaweed layer wrapping the rice, as in a traditional maki roll. The seaweed still proved too adventurous to an American clientele, who did not like to see it or chew it. Mr. Mashita, in true California innovative fashion, moved the seaweed roll on the inside and the rice on the outside —yet another bold experimentation! Out of this seasonal need and customer-driven adaptation, the first truly American sushi was born—the California roll!

The curious case of sushi adoption

By 2015 sushi business became a $2 billion industry in the United States. More than 4000 restaurants employed 25,000 people to serve sushi in the country. One can now buy sushi pre-packaged for lunch in disposable plastic dishes at grocery stores, at airport terminals wrapped in plastic and sold in open refrigerators, at sushi bars with conveyor belts endlessly circulating a wide selection in covered small plates, and at posh high-end restaurants artfully serving a colorful array of rolls on fine china. In cities like San Francisco and Seattle, you are never too far from a sushi serving joint. The comedian Jimmy Fallon funnily commented, "L.A., it's nice, but I think of sunshine and people on rollerblades eating sushi." In short, sushi has become a ubiquitous American food. The question then is how did this happen?

It is true that the Hollywood exposure and the California Roll, as described above, popularized sushi in the 1980s. But what is it that got the American early adopters to get hooked on this food in the first place?

To think of it, sushi is the unlikeliest of food to appeal to a western audience. First, it comes from a land that dragged the US into one of the bloodiest wars in history. In the 1940s and 1950s, one can safely say that Japan was not endearing to America. In 1941, the Empire of Japan attacked Pearl Harbor, scarring a nation with a date that would forever "live in infamy," as President Franklin Roosevelt put it. That act dragged the US into World War II. The war would cost 420,000 American lives, only ending after the US first developed and then dropped atomic bombs on two Japanese cities, instantly killing thousands of people. Some American G.I.s went so far as collecting and sending skulls of Japanese soldiers home to their loved ones as war trophies (a practice officially prohibited and condemned by the US military).

Beyond this forced historical gap, there was an inherent cultural gap between Japan and the US and that cultural gap extended to a culinary gap. Traditional sushi was very much at odds with an all-American meal of well-done steak served with mashed potatoes and gravy. First, sushi is fish, shellfish, octopus and other exotic sea creatures not common to the western palate. Second, it is mostly eaten raw! Next, there is little or no seasoning added—it is neither marinated nor brined beforehand. In fact, it is often served with cold rice and wrapped in seaweed. Accompaniments include pickled ginger and a very small assortment of odd sauces and mixtures: gari, wasabi, and soy sauce.

And as if it was not sufficient that the preparation and taste were peculiar, sushi is prepared and served by hand, often bare, and eaten with chopsticks. To an American audience obsessed with personal space and hygiene, touching somebody elses food with bare hands is almost sinful.

The question then remains—what was it that propelled sushi to bridge these seemingly insurmountable gaps and become so popular in the USA? I believe that eating sushi is more of an experience than filling one's belly.

Sukiyabashi Jiro

In April 2014, President Obama visited Japan. Prime Minister Shinzo Abe took President Obama out to dinner at a tiny restaurant called Sukiyabashi Jiro, located in a nondescript basement of an office building. The restaurant is as unconventional a restaurant as a restaurant can get. It has no Louis XIV furniture, no Picasso on the wall, no Beethoven playing in the background, no ornate mantles, no cathedral ceiling, no wine cellar, and above all, not even an elaborate menu. In fact, Sukiyabashi Jiro offers only one item on its menu—the omakase course consisting of twenty pieces of sushi prepared and served immediately.

Sukiyabashi Jiro is owned and operated by eighty-nine-year-old sushi master Jiro Ono. To Master Jiro, sushi is an art form. Making sushi is an art, serving sushi is an art, and consuming sushi is an art. That is why he personally makes the trip and picks out the freshest fish and other seafood from the market every morning. He has no set shopping list but buys what he feels is fresh that day. Along with a staff, that includes his sixty-year-old son, Master Jiro spends the day delicately preparing the food. This is a long process of cutting, cleaning, washing, and setting the raw ingredients the way countless generations of Japanese did in past centuries. The staff would spend forty-five minutes massaging the octopus for that day to bring out its best taste.

For the lucky guests who can get a seat at the restaurant (the average meal fare is $300 - $400), they are seated right in front of the master at the counter. In fact, the restaurant has only ten seats and cannot accommodate more guests at any one time. Master Jiro, standing behind the counter, observes the guests. He is as close to his guests as a chef can get. From this vantage point, he notices the finest details—who is sitting in which seat, who is right-handed or who is left-handed, who is in a happy mood or somber mood, who does the talking and who listens. Once the guests are ready, Master Jiro hand prepares the sushi pieces in the classic Tokyo style—combining the right amount of rice from a steamer box, slicing a piece of his chosen fish, adding some seasoning and maybe complementing with a small amount of soy sauce or nikiri. This preparation can appear very simple, but that would belie the master's almost samurai-like talent and precision to combine the perfect balance of flavors. This small bundle is the world's best-known sushi. Each guest is expected to eat the sushi right away as soon as the master serves it. The master, of course, decides what is served to which seated guest.

Sukiyabashi Jiro won the Michelin Guide three-star rating. In the restaurant industry, this is equivalent to winning the Lead Actor Oscar in Hollywood. Michelin Guide is the very well respected and oldest European restaurant and hotel guide and has been awarding stars for over one hundred years. When President Obama emerged from the restaurant, he claimed, "that's some good sushi right there. It was terrific."

Master Jiro spends hours purchasing and preparing the food daily. He stands in front of and very close to his ten customers and observes their every move. He does not have too many customers so he will not lose track of them. He focuses on a select few. He picks up on their moods, their chatter, and their laughter. He learns their behaviors by carefully observing cues. He looks for their receptions, their reactions, and their feelings. He then customizes the sushi right on the spot for them. He notices how they pick up the sushi, how they chew and swallow the food, and how they nod their heads or make facial gestures afterwards. He uses that feedback to prepare the next serving.

That level of care and attention places customers in a position of appreciation even if they may not necessarily like the food. The customer enjoys the overall activity and not just the food. The product that they are purchasing is not raw fish but a thrilling adventure customized for their utmost personal satisfaction. The chef is not selling food but is selling an ambience. The product does not only fulfill the hunger of the customer but fulfills deep-seated needs and desires to be respected and to be cared for. In short, Americans did not get addicted to raw fish but they got hooked on being pampered and treated well!

There are many lessons for any product here. If a product as unlikely as sushi can bridge such large gaps, one wonders what product cannot. As you launch yourself in the world as an entrepreneur or savvy business executive, remember the sushi lesson—you can turn any stinky fish in your product portfolio into a hit if you treat the customer right!

CHAPTER 4

HOW MUCH VALUE SHOULD I PLACE ON PRODUCT DESIGN?

*"You can design and create, and build the
most wonderful place in the world. But it
takes people to make the dream a reality."*
WALT DISNEY

*"A designer knows he has achieved perfection
not when there is nothing left to add, but
when there is nothing left to take away."*
ANTOINE DE SAINT-EXUPERY

*"Design is the fundamental soul of a man-made
creation that ends up expressing itself in successive outer
layers of the product or service. The iMac is not just
the color or translucence or the shape of the shell. The
essence of the iMac is to be the finest possible consumer
computer in which each element plays together."*
STEVE JOBS

O NCE, I INVITED SIX OF MY friends over for dinner. We dined and drank and bantered. We were all in a merry mood and we were having a pleasant time. At one point during dinner, I wanted to show them a video on YouTube. I pulled out my smart phone, navigated to YouTube, launched the video, and passed the phone over to the guest sitting next to me. He took the phone from me, grabbing it as we would all do—by clutching the two upper sides of the phone as I was holding the two lower sides of the phone. As soon as he picked up the phone this way, he inadvertently pressed the power button located on the top right side of the phone. The phone immediately went into locked mode. The guest passed the phone back to me and I had to unlock it, relaunch the video, and pass it back to him. This time, we were careful on how we both held the phone.

My first guest watched the video, had a good laugh, and then decided to pass the phone to the guest sitting next to him. And the exact same issue happened again! The second guest inadvertently locked the phone too and had to pass it back to me. This happened, I kid you not, with all of my six guests as the phone went around the table! And with each guest, my frustration was growing such that by the time the last guest watched the video, I was not in a laughing mood anymore! I was so disturbed by this incident—how the simple bad positioning of a button on a phone could ruin a happy experience with friends—that I decided to invite six executives from this mobile phone company for dinner!

I had the six executives from the company, which happens to be the largest competitor to Apple's iPhone, sit around the table in the same manner my close friends sat. The executives, of course, were not aware that they were here for a blind test of their own product. Part-way through dinner, I pulled my smart phone out, launched YouTube, and played the video. I then passed the phone to the company executive next to me. Guess what happened? If you guessed that he held the phone by its upper sides, you are wrong! He carefully took the phone from my hands by clasping the bottom sides of the phone. I was dumbfounded! After he watched the video, I asked him to pass the phone to the guest next to him. Again, surprise! The second guest picked up the phone without pressing the power button. As the phone made its way around the table this time, none of the phone company executives inadvertently turned off the phone. When the phone came back to me, I informed them of their behavior and explained to them that it was unlike the behavior of their typical customers. They told me that they knew of the side button design flaw but somehow it was not their problem to solve. They assigned the blame for the problem to somebody else—but, they were unsure exactly who to blame! Hence, instead of fixing the design, employees at the company had changed their own behavior, all the while expecting somebody else to fix the issue. Over time, they conditioned themselves to not experience and not see the design problem altogether.

In fact, I would argue that this problem has propagated. The side buttons are very sensitive to the touch. By just holding the phone, I am always inadvertently changing the volume. This is very irritating as I now find myself having to readjust my phone volume every time I pick up or make a call. But, it gets even worse! That sensitive side button also acts as a shutter button when the phone is in the camera mode. God knows how many times my phone has taken pictures by itself! Not only were the managers at this company selling a product with a design flaw, they had trapped themselves in an environment where they could not see, and hence could not fix, the flaw. Of course, Apple iPhones, on the other hand, have always located the power button on the top side of the phone.

In subsequent phone designs, the Korean company added a soft back button next to the home key. I have found this "magic" back button to be extremely useful. It allows the user to quickly access her recent functions. In fact, I observed other users of the device making use of that back button a lot too. I have noticed that the back button is the location with the most fingerprints on these users' phones. It is unconceivable for Apple to add this second button as they favor a sparse design. And, if you hand over an iPhone to a user of the Korean phone, the user would unconsciously look for that non-existent back button on the phone as he interacts with the phone—it is funny to see.

On the other hand, this Korean phone company has to get credit for taking a risk on the market and releasing a phone with a larger screen size at the same time that most phones were getting smaller. All of a sudden, mobile commerce started to outpace Web commerce. I wonder—did it all start with the larger phone screen size?

How do companies know if they have designed a product well? How many risks should they take with design? How much should they innovate? How can they avoid a groupthink trap?

Apple's DNA

In February 2015, Apple Inc. achieved a feat that no other company in the history of American public companies has ever achieved. Its market capitalization, calculated by multiplying the number of outstanding shares and the price per share, crossed the $700 billion mark. In fact, Apple's revenue of $58 billion in the first quarter of 2015 was $14 billion more than the quarterly revenue of Microsoft, Google, Yahoo and Facebook combined. Apple's balance of cash and marketable securities was $193.5 billion—$13.5 billion more than the combined total cash of the other four companies. And Apple is achieving such unbelievable revenue metrics with a fairly parse line of products. Compared to its competitors, they sell a high quantity of the same products. Apple's high share price reflects the confidence of investors, not only in its present success, but also in the company's continuing domination of its industry in the quarters ahead. Apple clearly has left its competitors in the dust as it speeds forward to a promising future. The company appears to be untouchable.

The question that comes naturally to a company that has enjoyed such tremendous success is "what are they are doing differently when compared to their competitors?" Apple is a technology company. Could it be that they are the first to invent new technologies in spaces unexplored? Consider this: Apple released its first iPhone in 2007. Motorola, the cell-phone pioneer, released its first commercial handheld cellular phone, the Motorola DynaTAC phone, in 1984—twenty-three years before Apple! Despite this very long technological lead, Motorola is today a shadow of its former self and is part of Lenovo. Apple, on the other hand, is worth more than the gross national product of the entire country of Switzerland.

We see a similar pattern with many other Apple products and technologies—the company does not rush head first into technology spaces. While being a technology company, they do not solely rely on technology. Steve Jobs summarized Apple's ethos as follows: "It is in Apple's DNA that technology alone is not enough—it's technology married with liberal arts, married with the humanities, that yields us the results that make our heart sing." In other words, the product's overall design is core to its success.

Product Design is the process of turning ideas into articles for use. Without design, ideas will remain just that —concepts in our minds. With sub-optimal design, great ideas can be turned into mediocre products. It is only with delicate, thoughtful, and creative design that we can turn great ideas into great products. And the best designs imbibe a combination of art, science, and technology with the end customer always in mind. Let us repeat this: great products are a combination of great ideas and the best design. And the best design optimizes the use of art, science, and technology without losing sight of the customer's needs.

Apple's products beautifully reflect this mix and Steve Jobs best exemplifies the executive who understood this ideal. Apple's trailblazing success can be directly attributed to the huge appeal its products design has to its legion of customers. Having said that, Apple should not rest on its laurels. To maintain their market lead, their unprecedented revenue streams, and their customer base, they need to remain true to these design ideals. It remains to be seen if future CEOs of Apple will be as visionary as Steve Jobs and whether they will carry on his legacy.

The least likely big hit

Let us now look at a how good design can turn a product as boring as a thermostat into a hit product. In 2001, Apple Inc. introduced the digital jukebox with "1000 songs in your pocket," the iPod. That precursor to the iPhone revolutionized the music industry in more ways than one. First, the product sped the adoption of a new manner to sell music through the accompanying software and online store, iTunes—selling one song at a time instead of whole tracks, like on a cassette tape or CD, from the same artist. That single innovation upended the traditional music industry and shook up media distribution power structures that have been in place for over a century, while placing more control in the hands of song writers and performers. Next, the product had an easy to use "column" software interface based on Apple's operating system. The interface was easy to navigate and very intuitive. But, the most profound feature of the iPod was its beautiful hardware design. Its glossy white interface would go on to define the clean and simple look of Apple products. The smooth rounded edges made it comfortable in every palm holding it. The accompanying long and sleek earphone wires, at a time when Bluetooth wireless technology was to lead the industry into an era of no wires, would become a fad for all, from teenagers to joggers to fashionistas. But, its most noticeable appeal was the "wheel" —a touch interface control that allowed scrolling and navigating the songs content of the device with a one thumb. The wheel gave the user an almost mystical, soothing satisfaction scrolling with one finger in a circular motion—when compared to the whole hand mouse operation of a PC. It was a design that would usher in a paradigm shift in user interfaces. Critics initially wrote off the iPod, but that design would turn it into an instant success paving the way to all the future Apple handheld devices. That iPod design was the brainchild of Tony Fadell working directly under Steve Jobs' supervision.

Tony Fadell would have a very unique relationship with Steve Jobs, a relationship characterized by Fortune Magazine as one "that alternated between the father/son and school principal/ naughty student archetypes." He would be groomed by the Master himself. Jobs and Fadell had many things in common—they were both repeat entrepreneurs who had faced failures, they were both biological sons of Middle Eastern immigrant fathers, and they were both consummate idealists when it came to the nitty-gritty details of product design. By 2008, rumors were flying in Silicon Valley that the "godfather of the iPod" was the likely next CEO of Apple. However, ambitious large personalities always chart their own courses. To everybody's surprise, that year Fadell decided to leave Apple.

He spent the next several months consumed with the construction of his vacation home near Lake Tahoe. While working on this decidedly non-technological project, he realized that there were plenty of devices around the home that he could reinvent with the latest technological advances. He decided to start with the thermostat! In 2010, he returned to Silicon Valley and launched Nest Labs.

The thermostat ought to be the least likely device a successful technology entrepreneur in Silicon Valley would want to spend time on. It was the product of the last century's companies, which were headquartered far from the West Coast—companies like Honeywell, Trane, and Carrier. It was a boring device that simply turned heat or cold air on or off. It was not much more than a square digital clock! However, Fadell had a vision. He saw the device from completely different angles. And, he started with a different design.

The Nest thermostat is as elegant in design as the first iPod. First, it is everything that a regular thermostat is not. It is circular like the original iPod control and not rectangular in shape. The circular structure comprises of an outer wheel that rotates and an inner screen interface that is fixed. It replaces several push buttons with no button—one simply pushes the wheel to select. The user scrolls through its interface by rotating the outer wheel of the device—giving the user the same pleasant satisfaction of circular motion rather than pushing on multiple plastic buttons. The rotation is paired with audible clicks as one rotates the wheel making the experience realistic. The software interface is intuitive and easy to navigate. The device is, of course, Internet-connected and supported by a clean Web-based user portal and dashboard. But Fadell went further in realizing his design. He ensured that the installation of the device could be done in only a few simple steps without the expertise of a professional electrician—every homeowner with a screwdriver could install the thermostat in a matter of minutes. And, to make matters even easier, he included an ergonomic screwdriver in the box. Fadell also included a wall plate along with the screw-driver. Now, you may be asking—what is a wall plate and what does it have to do with the thermostat? The wall plate is a beautiful metal base on which the Nest thermostat can be mounted, in case the user damages the wall while removing his old thermostat. Fadell designed this product combining the elements we discussed—art, science, and technology with the customer in mind!

With this one product transformed from boring to sexy, Nest Labs became an instant Silicon Valley phenomenon. It would unsettle the incumbents. Honeywell's reaction was to sue Nest Labs for patent infringement. But, it would also attract the right attention —among investors and venture capitalists. Nest Labs became the avant-garde of companies developing Internet-of-Things products and it would inspire countless startups trying to reinvent home automation. In 2014, Google acquired Nest Labs for $3.2 billion.

Design is the entrepreneur's craft through which ideas are brought to life. It is similar to the artist sculpting a piece of rock. It requires delicate, thoughtful, and almost compassionate handi-ness. It requires knowledge of what to remove and what to keep, what to blunt and what to smooth, what to hide and what to bring out. Get it wrong and you just molded a pile of pebbles. Get it right and you may just create the next Picasso.

Learning from the honeycomb

In 36 BC, the Roman soldier, scholar, and writer Marcus Terentius Varro remarked that the distinct, near-perfect hexagonal shape of the honeycomb cell is no design accident; the shape must have a very definite purpose. Varro conjectured that the regular hexagonal shape (i.e., with sides of equal length) of the honeycomb cells is the best way to divide a surface into regions of equal area with the least total perimeter. Two thousand years later, MIT Professor and Physicist Alan Lightman mathematically proved the conjecture to be true. Throughout history, the honeycomb has been called a natural design marvel. Charles Darwin said it "is absolutely perfect in economizing labor and wax."

The honeycomb cells are arranged in regular hexagons because first, this structure minimizes gaps in between the cells and avoids wasted space. Next, it allows the honeybees to work simultaneously, rather than sequentially, when building the cells and hence avoids wasting time. The smallest total perimeter of the sides means that the smallest amount of wax is needed by the bees to construct the honeycomb. For every ounce of wax, a bee must consume about eight ounces of honey. This translates into multiple visits outside of the hive to hundreds of flowers. By minimizing the perimeter of the cells, and hence the amount of wax needed, the bees are minimizing effort and expense of energy. In short, the honeycomb is a design that is scientifically sound and technologically efficient. It is also artistically beautiful. The regular, repeated, and symmetrical patterns of the cells are a visual delight. The golden liquid bubbles filling the cells, glistening in ray of lights, with the promise of the rich taste of honey conjures a picture of art at its finest.

Leonardo da Vinci, observing nature, commented "Human subtlety...will never devise an invention more beautiful, more simple, or more direct than does nature, because in her inventions nothing is lacking, and nothing is superfluous." Hence, nature is our ultimate teacher of design.

We can reflect on the honeycomb and ask ourselves many illuminating questions about good product design.

IS THE DESIGN SIMPLE ENOUGH?

Leonardo da Vinci was also known to have said, "Simplicity is the ultimate form of sophistication." It is difficult to be simple. And, it is very easy to get complicated. Adding is easy. Removing is hard. Great design strives to be simple, natural and elegant. It is easy on the eye and easy on the emotions. It makes use of symmetry and avoids un-natural shapes. It extends nature's design and extends the human form. Great design is ergonomic. It is inviting and does not force itself on the user. It is not incongruent with its intended surroundings. Simple design takes note of its environment and as such it is environmentally friendly and green. Great design is simple and fits in seamlessly.

IS THE DESIGN INTUITIVE?

How many times do we open a product package, put the manual on the side, pick up the product and fiddle with it hoping that it will work? Now how many times does the product fail to work because we cannot figure out how to operate it? I have seen and have experienced these situations countless times. The more people struggle to make the product work, the more they get frustrated and the more they get frustrated the higher the likelihood that they will not like the product, return the product or not buy from the same company again. An unintuitive design for a product is a certain way to irritate a customer! Good design is intuitive. It makes sense right away. If part of the design is complex, there are simple cues like colored buttons, familiar shapes, arrows, etc., to guide the user. Intuitive design is instinctive – the user does not need to be trained to use the product. Intuitive design does not require a manual.

IS THE DESIGN BEAUTIFUL?

"Things are pretty, graceful, rich, elegant, handsome, but, until they speak to the imagination, not yet beautiful", wrote Ralph Waldo Emerson. Beautiful design captures the imagination. It is design that triggers the emotions of satisfaction, contentment and mild pleasure in the user. It is design that initiates an unconscious smile and a sense of curiosity. It is design that seduces the user to spend more time with the product. It evokes a timeless sense of appreciation because the design is seen as art. As such, beautiful design has all the elements that make great art.

Consider the clay pots of early African tribes – they are made in an elaborate, often ritual process, they are shaped symmetrically and they are decorated with painted patterns. These design choices do not necessarily improve the basic function of the pots, which may be to store water. Or, these design choices are not the most cost effective way to make the product. However, they allow the owner and user of the product to connect to the product in a more human and personal way. We have to be careful when designing modern products not to be only focused on economic efficiency. Often times, by doing so we design beauty out and we come up with an economical but unappealing product. As humans, we cannot help loving what is beautiful. And no product should be designed unless expressed effort is made to ensure that it looks, feels and sounds beautiful.

IS THE DESIGN INNOVATIVE?

To design is to create. And to create is to innovate. Good design comes up with something new and something different, rather than repeat an existing form. Good design offers an improvement, an amelioration, or an addition. It is novel and different. Innovative design captures our attention, draws out our curiosity, and satiates our fascination. Innovative design pushes the envelope in that it challenges the norm. It is risky. Innovative design requires the creative genius of its author. Innovative design influences the environment around it. The renowned author and philosopher Marshall McLuhan once said that, "We shape our tools and thereafter our tools shape us." Innovative design shapes our life for the better.

IS THE DESIGN HOLISTIC?

Good design considers the system as an interconnected whole. Good design evaluates each part of the system individually, looks at how they fit together, and assesses the resulting end product. Holistic design looks at the larger picture without losing sight of the details. It is comprehensive and detailed. Holistic design emphasizes and synergizes the parts. It is design that results in a sum that is larger than the parts. Holistic design integrates the look and feel of the overall product. It considers the emotions of users whether they are looking at one angle or one component of the product or whether they have a bird's eye view of the overall product. Holistic design ensures that each and every part of the product works together, works well, and works seamlessly (as Steve Jobs liked to say). It emphasizes the functional relationships of every part. Holistic design brings an almost spiritual yin-yang balance to each part, making a whole that is naturally at peace with itself and with its environment.

DOES THE DESIGN BALANCE WISH AND NEED?

Good design satisfies both the desires and needs of the customer. It considers what the user would like to have as well as what the user has to have. It solves an immediate problem and gives hope about an upcoming better solution. It has an element of the present as well as the future in it. It is immediately gratifying while being visionary and futuristic. Good design extends the product over time, builds a lasting relationship with the customer and points to a bright future.

I believe Elon Musk's Tesla Motors achieves this on many levels. The game-changing Tesla Model S satisfies an immediate need for the commuter as well as an ultimate desire to be energy efficient and go green for the environmentally conscious customer. The electric car does not sacrifice on interior size (it is a five-door luxury sedan) or on exterior shape (it is stylish and critics rave over the beautiful design). It is not inefficient—in fact, it won numerous awards, including *Consumer Reports'* top-scoring car ever and *Car and Driver's* Car of the Century! While fulfilling, even exceeding, all the functions of a luxury sedan, the Model S also incites a desire to create a more responsible future in its customers. The car is as much a statement to be Earth-friendly, energy-conscious and socially-responsible as it is a vehicle. It is both useful and hopeful. And in 2017, Tesla's stock surpassed GM, making Tesla the most valuable car maker in America.

IS THE DESIGN FUNCTIONAL?

A famous Steve Jobs-ism is "It just works!" Good design just works. It makes a product functional, useful, and efficient. Functional design does not fail. Good design produces a predictable, stable, and satisfactory output whenever the product is used. It is also repeatable. The user depends on the design to work and takes it for granted that it will work when needed. Soon, the product abstracts into the background, not interfering with the life of the user but yet produces the desired function that benefits the user. Functional design does not stress the user about the possibility of product failures. Let us take an example—a well-designed light bulb, when turned on, provides ample ambient light that illuminates and soothes a room. The user does not have to worry about whether the light bulb may or may not work, whether the amount of light will or will not be sufficient, whether it will be distracting, etc. Rather, the light bulb works, remains in the background, and yet provides the user an indispensable function.

DOES THE DESIGN ADD VALUE?

In addition to being functional, i.e., working as expected, design benefits the user—it adds value. Good design confers an advantage over other alternatives. It benefits the customer more and it establishes a competitive edge for the manufacturer. This in turn makes it profitable to both the owner and the manufacturer. The return for the customer on the good design is far more than the cost of acquiring the design in the first place. And the manufacturer can charge a premium for good design over competitors' alternatives. Good design improves performance, reduces costs, saves times, and eliminates liability. Good design is utile—it provides some measure of positive utility to its owners, whether in terms of economic utility, emotional utility, or psychological utility.

IS THE DESIGN PARTICIPATORY?

Good design comes together by synergizing ideas from multiple parties. Multiple designers may work on one single design, each contributing ideas towards a better final product. It is smart to hire a cross-section of people from diverse background, experiences, and cultures into a design team. It is well-known that better ideas are brought out by having a diverse group brainstorming and collaborating on a problem rather than have one single person track down a solution. Good design coopts the voice of the customer. It comes to fruition with suggestions and feedback from the customers. Many software companies release beta versions of their products, use the customers' feedback, and then improve the next release. Good design is participatory. It considers all sides. Good design breaks narrow, groupthink mentality but blends ideas of many in a harmonious and balanced product.

IS THE DESIGN SATISFYING?

And in the end, good design satisfies various needs for the customer—functional needs, economic needs, aesthetics needs and emotional needs. Good design leaves the customer in a better state of mind and in a better mood whenever it is used. Good design brings joy to and improves the quality of life of the customer. The customer loves to experience the design and once away from the design, desires to come back and use it again. Good design delights the customer!

The honeycomb is certainly a design marvel—one that blends art, science, and technology, or aesthetics, principles, and functions. However, the honeycomb exists only because of the assiduous work of the honeybee—a habit and an ethic that this tiny, yet indispensable, insect cultivated over thousands of years. Are you willing to work as hard and as diligently as the honeybee to achieve this level of perfection? Are you able to work long years and very patiently just to get one product right? Are you willing to discover and consider all the elements necessary? Perfection in design makes all the difference.

CHAPTER 5

WHY WOULD I NEED MORE THAN ONE CAR KEY?

"Any product that needs a manual to work is broken."
ELON MUSK

*"Build a better mousetrap, and the world
will beat a path to your door."*
RALPH WALDO EMERSON

"I don't design clothes, I design dreams."
RALPH LAUREN

VISITING NEW PLACES, MEETING diverse people, capturing life moments with my camera are among my few
great passions. My travels naturally begin and end at airports around the world. It is a sad fact that an amazing experience
in a foreign country can quickly be ruined by a bad experience at
their airport. It is even sadder when I note that the bad experience
in these airports is usually due to simple issues that can be fixed
with thoughtful and good design.

I have been to several airports in Asia where it is harder to
push the luggage cart around than to actually pull my own suit-
case! The technology for luggage carts comprises a platform sitting on a set of wheels that transfers force making it easy to move
heavier loads on the platform. Sounds complex? This is the same
technology invented when bullocks were pulling ox carts in the
field hundreds of years ago. Why is it then that luggage carts at
many airports invariably still have wheels that don't turn, that are
squeaky, and that don't even touch the ground? Why is it hard to
load and unload the carts? Why is it hard to start pushing the carts
and once in motion, is it even harder to stop the carts? Why is it
so hard to navigate the carts along the winding corridors of the
airports? Why do the authorities spend so much in building large
airports and yet cannot spend an insignificant amount of money
on improving their luggage carts?

They, of course, do not have the customer's experience in
mind. The very carts that are supposed to ease my efforts to move
luggage always leave me drained and fatigued! All the issues I mentioned are simple to fix with proper design. In fact, these issues are
now being fixed at many other airports around the world. It took

thirty years for the management of these airports to realize this simple design flaw! It is common now to see carts designed with ergonomic shapes, wheels with ball bearings, double handles that serve as brakes when released, made with light metal such as aluminum, etc.

Another of my pet peeves at many airports has been the need to carry a boarding pass. A boarding pass is a piece of unnecessary paper that determines whether you get on your plane or not. Once issued, you have to carry it around with fastidious precaution. As if traveling was not already stressful, now you have to make sure that this piece of paper that you cannot fold, that does not fit in your pocket or wallet, and that has to be hand carried while you are also pushing carts and holding handbags always remain in your possession! If you ever lose your boarding pass, be prepared to explain yourself across language barriers to unsympathetic airport security officers—not a pleasant encounter! I have been advocating for years to either simplify the boarding pass into a magnetic credit card sized, wallet-friendly card or to get rid of it altogether, replaced by electronic passes on your mobile devices. Both of these are design choices as the technology is simple to implement. Only recently have airports, especially in the West, adopted electronic boarding passes.

Luggage carts and boarding passes are only two of many personal vexations I have with airports around the world. Looking around me, I wish airport management would redesign walkways, lighting, indication signs, baggage claims, conveyor belts, transportation, immigration counters, security checks, x-ray scanners, and the list goes on! It is ironic that many governments would spend billions of dollars building large airports and then spend billions of dollars more marketing their countries to attract tourists and yet, due to simple design flaws, they create very negative experiences at their airports. There is no worse experience for a tourist than starting a vacation or ending a vacation with a bad taste in one's mouth!

More than tech products

In the previous chapter, we looked at how design is critical to the latest technological products on the market, like the mobile phone with the side button flaw, the Apple iPod and iPhone, and the Nest Labs thermostat. It is easy to make the case to put great design into a new product that is being launched for the first time. But, what about old, non-technological products that have been around for a long time, products that are working just fine and have been well adopted by large numbers of customers? Does the same definition of good design, as one that combines art, science, and technology, apply to non-technology products, say, shopping carts at the supermarket or luggage carts at the airport? Should we try and redesign products, like doorknobs, which have worked fine for many years? Isn't changing the design of an old product only adding costs while not necessarily increasing revenue?

New technology products differentiate from one another on many variables. First, they have many components. Take the iPhone and Galaxy examples. The two phones compete on screen size and resolution, memory and storage size, placement and number of cameras, lens megapixels, processor speed, battery life, operating systems performance, etc. Second, the phones are part of larger ecosystems of other third-party factors, such as availability of apps, carrier networks, accessories, etc. They are also offered at different price points, service plans, and warranties. All these factors have some influence on the overall performance and appeal of the phones. Customers deciding between these two technology products would weigh the pros and cons of both in their decision-making process and choose the phone they deem to have a better performance or greater appeal.

Now, compare this to a commodity product, like a doorknob. Doorknobs from two different manufacturers would likely have similar components and similar levels of performance since they have already been optimized for their intended functions a long time ago. The classical definition of a commodity, such as a doorknob, is a "class of goods for which there is demand but which is supplied without qualitative differentiation across a market." In other words, commodities are not differentiated on their features. Commodities are characterized by another economic reality—their price points do not vary by much. How can we then differentiate between commodities? The most important factor that differentiates commodities, like doorknobs, is actually their design. Absent new technological development, design is the most critical differentiator for products that have been around for a long time.

What features do your customers really care about?

In my early days in the United States, I bought my first car, a Chevy Malibu! The car had a lot of nice features—it was stylish and pleasing to look at, it was roomy on the inside, it had a feeling of toughness and durability to it, and it drove fine. This American icon allowed me to experience my new adopted country with all its superlatives—the car was bigger, bolder, and stronger than any other car I drove back in Korea.

However, the smallest details in its design somehow prevented me from fully enjoying this new experience. And one minor detail upset me most—the car came with a set of two different keys and each key was double-sided with different ridge configurations on the two sides. What this means is that the two keys could open four locks depending on which key and which side was used. One key would serve as the ignition key and start the engine and then would open the doors when turned around and inserted into the door lock. The other key would open the trunk and the gas cap. Worse, the keys were thin and brittle and would break often.

Now, you may wonder how can a set of two keys be a cause of complaint when it hardly impacted the driving experience of the car. Consider this: every American household owns two to three cars. In a household with three Chevy Malibus, you would need to carry six almost identical keys in your pocket. Now imagine this common scene in suburban America: a mother of three young children running back from the grocery store with two big bags of groceries and kids in tow in a rainy parking lot trying to figure out which key can open her Chevy car door! As she fumbles with the keys, tries one key, tries one side, gets frustrated for picking the wrong key/side combination and tries again, she could only swear at the engineers who designed this solution. All the while, she is juggling the grocery bags and is worried that her crying kids will be catching a cold and would miss school the next day!

At that moment, does the customer appreciate the stylish tail fins of the Chevy or does she simply want to find the right key to open the car door and get her kids to safety? Now, ask yourself—how much time did the Chevy engineers put into designing the tail fins with its beautiful lights and how much time would it have taken them to design a single key that would open all doors, trunk, and start the car engine? Simple design choices eliminate customer frustration.

At around the same time, Japanese auto manufacturers were shipping cars to the United States. They had detected this design flaw and had fixed the problem. In fact, Japanese cars were focused on the customer experience. I have a friend who recounted to me how pleased he was when he bought a Honda Odyssey after the birth of his second child. He was surprised at all the amenities the minivan came with for a young parent with two little children. The van, for example, had a dedicated rearview mirror for the driving parent to keep watch of the kids sitting in the rear. The van had separate rear and front audio controls so that the kids can sleep quietly at the back while the parents enjoy music in the front. Its automatic side doors came with shades or curtains to keep the little ones from the glare of the sun. Now, these are features that are common to most cars or minivans serving this demographic today. But, it was not always so. The Japanese manufacturers clearly had a lead in such designs around the customer needs over the American manufacturers. From the 1980s to the 2000s, is it a surprise then that the Japanese auto industry challenged the American auto industry, leading to its near collapse and government bailouts?

Now fast forward to 2015. According to Bloomberg News, the National Highway Traffic Safety Administration (NHTSA) had logged more than 18,000 complaints about key ignitions. They involve multiple models and carmakers and range from keys getting stuck, vehicles stalling at high speeds, and even cars starting on their own. The key could be inadvertently jarred by a knee, uneven road, or weighed down by a heavy key chain. General Motors, which owns the Chevrolet brand, was under investigation because it was aware of these issues and waited more than a decade to recall the affected cars.

Mary Barra, CEO of GM, made a formal apology for how her company handled the complaints regarding ignition switches over the past decade. Since being appointed as CEO early in 2014, Ms. Barra has appeared in front of Congress, the press, and the public multiple times to explain how her company had failed to properly address issues with the ignition switch. And in 2015, GM agreed to pay $900 million as part of the Justice Department investigation into its failure to fix the deadly ignition-switch defect blamed for more than 120 deaths. U.S. Attorney Preet Bharara left the door open to prosecuting specific GM employees.

Good design that makes use of art, science, and technology is at the heart of great customer experience. Design is especially important for products that are common across many competitors and that lack the power to differentiate solely based on their components and performance. Design is a small cost in the grander scheme of things. A bad luggage cart ruins a traveler's experience even when the airport cost billions of dollars to build. A single set of car keys does not frustrate a customer and could avert deadly accidents. And, a good coffeemaker signs up a hotel guest for her next visit.

Good design is particularly important to commodities—probably even more so than for technology products. To optimize your customer experience and maximize your revenue, you need to pay particular attention to the design of every element of your products, irrespective of whether you sell burgers from a food truck or water faucets for the bathroom.

CHAPTER 6

HOW CAN I BE SURE MY CUSTOMER SERVICE STRATEGY WORKS?

"The goal as a company is to have customer service that is not just the best but legendary."

SAM WALTON

"Your most unhappy customers are your greatest source of learning."

BILL GATES

"You've got to start with the customer experience and work back toward the technology—not the other way around."

STEVE JOBS

"A customer is the most important visitor on our premises, he is not dependent on us. We are dependent on him. He is not an interruption in our work. He is the purpose of it. He is not an outsider in our business. He is part of it. We are not doing him a favor by serving him. He is doing us a favor by giving us an opportunity to do so."

MAHATMA GANDHI

WHEN I TRAVELED AROUND Asia back in the 1980s, I always considered Japan the leader in department store management. However, things have changed and Korea is now the reigning champion. Now Japan management should go visit Korea and relearn some lessons!

But once upon a time I experienced great customer service in department stores across Japan. I enjoy going out shopping early in the day and I always noticed something distinct occurring in department stores a few minutes before they open. As I peered in through the window from the outside, I'd see the employees all dressed up impeccably, lining up in the store. The manager would walk in front of them and lead them in a chorus. They, in unison, uttered the company motto, pumped their fists in the air, and shouted their dedication to make the coming day a better day for themselves, their families, their employer, and their customers. Once rallied, the employees opened the store doors and treated their customers with utmost care and respect. The store itself had been impeccably cleaned and readied, all items neatly arranged and placed at eye level. The store was set up such that it was easy to maneuver around items even with a large cart, soft music playing in the background, and each employee carried a smile. The environment itself warmly invited the customers in and made them feel very comfortable. No doubt, customers enjoyed visiting these stores! As odd as such a routine may appear to a Western audience, it clearly had a positive impact on sales and customer service. The ritual grounded and aligned everybody in the shop or office around a common objective first thing at the start of the day. Many different businesses across Asia have adopted a similar morning staff rallying routine.

Contrast this with the bad customer service by some in the hospitality industry, who also assume they will automatically be tipped. Don't get me wrong, I believe in tipping for good service. Here, I am not referring to a tip jar being placed on a counter at your neighborhood coffee shop, but rather the unspoken demand of service providers, such as the luggage handler at the hotel, who wait with anticipation to be tipped. When expectations to be tipped get close to becoming a demand for tips, it is a distraction for the employee and an annoyance for the customer. I have experienced many such attitudes over the years—a hotel clerk who insists on finding some problems with the hotel room, a luggage handler at the airport who insists on carrying my light briefcase, or a server at a restaurant who interrupts every few minutes asking about the quality of the food. It seems at times that the expectation for tipping has gotten out of control and everyone expects a tip: waiters, baristas, servers, baggage handlers, busboys, babysitters, aestheticians, hair dressers, entertainers, cab drivers, valets, and the list goes on!

When the expectation to be tipped is so strong as to make the customer uncomfortable, it is not good customer service but rather a disservice. It is important that companies provide an incentive to employees to be rewarded irrespective of the tips they receive. Tips cannot be the sole mode of compensation for the employees because then their primary objective will be to extract as much money as they can from the customer. Their attempt to maximize service can become a nuisance instead of a positive experience!

Now, let us look at banks in Asia. Banks in Asia are generally known for their bureaucratic processes. They are also known for the unfriendliness of their management—again as if lending money to a customer is doing the customer a great favor. You need to make an appointment to see the manager, then wait in line or wait for a long time for no apparent reason, and then be received in a back room by a glum-looking, often angry manager. Lower-ranked employees live in fear of their bosses and treat the customers with the same attitude of disregard that their bosses do. Often times, people who may be seeking a bank service are already stressed. This type of atmosphere just makes the customer feel even worse. And, as we have seen previously, companies where customers work to serve their bosses and not the end customers are doomed to fail.

Compare this to banks in the US where the managers sit right up front, close to the entrance to welcome their customers with a big smile. Cashiers are trained to chitchat with the customers, ask them about their children and how their day is going, and treat them like a friendly neighbor. Staffers always treat their customers first and do not have to live in fear of their bosses watching over them.

Similarly, many airlines go the extra mile to keep their customers happy. We have already seen how Southwest Airlines in the US treat their customers well. But, many airlines worldwide have realized that increased profits go hand-in-hand with good customer service. The airline industry is an industry with cutthroat competition and several companies have realized that the only way to stay afloat is to attract and retain customers. I am always appreciative of the services provided by Emirates Airlines and Qatar Airways. They have clearly placed the satisfaction of their customers at the very top on their priority list and are able to train their employees to execute accordingly.

Singapore Airlines, which is repeatedly ranked among the top airlines in the world, has very good service: the carrier has a very friendly crew, the food service is excellent, the entertainment program is well varied, and the onboard manual keeps the customer engaged. I personally believe that they still have room to improve. Many planes in their fleet are old and as such the amenities do not fully cater to the modern day traveler. In one such older plane, I found that the privacy in the business class was lacking and the entertainment hardware was quite old. Even on the ground, I once waited two weeks to get them to retrieve information on my frequent flyer membership.

The British Virgin Group, led by Sir Richard Branson, is also famous for its high level of customer service. Their airlines division is built on the concept of youthful fun. Everything from their choice of colors inside the cabins to how passengers order drinks to the food they serve to the cheerful vibe of their flight attendants keeps the happy customer experience as the most important objective. In fact, Sir Richard Branson himself personifies the image of Virgin—he is a fun-chasing, always smiling, customer-pleasing, risk-taker.

Customer service seems so clearly related to business success. So why is it so hard for companies to prioritize and maintain high customer service?

Before, during, and after

Customer service is taking care of the customer's needs and desires by providing and delivering professional, helpful, high quality service and assistance during the *whole* experience of a transaction. Customer service can take the form of an in-person interaction, a courtesy call, an assistance call, self-service systems such as kiosks, web-based interaction, follow-up emails, public forums, one-on-one chat, as it is the experience that the customer remembers. It is an interaction with the customer where the company listens to the customer and improves the customer's delight with the company, its representatives, its products, and its services.

Customer service starts even before customers know they have a certain need that needs to be fulfilled. The elderly may not notice that climbing a set of stairs is getting harder with age. The smart company understands the aging profile of its customer base and rethinks its products standards and specifications to make the steps that it sells a few millimeters shorter to require less exertion to climb. Demographic trends are only one set of factors that a smart company monitors. It should also monitor general economic trends, political trends, social trends, and technology trends. If globalization is forcing cultures together, for example, then the smart company can know what the next generation's needs will be, how different these needs are from the current generation's needs, and how the products and services need to be altered to meet such needs.

Customer service picks up when customers formulate the idea that they need a certain service or product. If a customer logs into a computer and looks for a certain solution to a problem, the smart company immediately understands that there is a need someone is trying to fulfill and serves the right information to arrive at a genuine solution for the customer. If a customer walks into a mall, make the customer feel welcome. Note that at this stage the company needs to provide unbiased information to the customer, make the customer feel comfortable, and empower the customer to make the right choice. Do not oversell at this stage since the customer has not made a purchase decision yet. Rather, provide the customer with useful and empowering information. A customer who receives neutral and useful information from a company will trust that company and trust always leads to strong long-term relationships.

Customer service accelerates when the customer chooses to consider the company's products. That could be a decision by the customer to visit a company store or web site. The customer at this stage is still searching for the best solution but is considering the company's offerings as a viable option. For that consideration alone, the company ought to be grateful and serve the customer. Again, do not oversell to the customer but rather enable the customer to make the right choice from his point of view. Progressive Auto Insurance gives customers who are seeking insurances quotes from its own offerings as well as from offerings of its competitors. Remember, customer service is serving the customer's needs and not the company's needs.

Customer service picks up full speed when the customer decides to purchase the company's products or services. At this point, a customer has made the decision to spend money on your products and as such he needs to feel that he is receiving the best value for the money he is spending. Customer service is not limited to providing a good product but it encompasses the whole transactional experience between the customer, sales associate, cashier, customer service agent, website or kiosk. Customer service includes the manner a company representative talks to the customer, the amount of time the customer waits before he is attended to, the comfort level of the store which includes everything from the display of the products to the ambient temperature, to favorable lighting and inviting seats, to the ease of payment and the packaging and bagging of the merchandise. And, of course, saying, "thank you" with a smile at the end.

Customer service does not end when the customer walks out of the store. Indeed, customer service cruises when the customer takes the product home for use for decades to come or decides to return the product the very next day. A company should try and follow-up with a customer. Some doctors and dentists in the USA will call their patients in the evening after seeing the patients during the day just to make sure that the patients are okay. Some car dealers will call customers within 30 days to make sure that the purchased vehicles are working with no problem. And should the customer decide to return the product, per the return policy, do not make it a fuss to take the product back. Instead, use the occasion to learn what are the reasons the customer returned the products, what could be improved, and whether the customer can be serviced by a different and better product.

It's not always transferrable

It is also important to realize that customer service should be designed specifically for the customer whom your business is serving. Sometimes, executives try to carry over an approach that worked with customers at their previous companies because it was successful there, not realizing that the customer needs often vary across businesses. Ron Johnson was hired from Apple to lead JC Penney, the American retail giant, after a major push by activist shareholder Bill Ackman in 2011. Ron Johnson is credited for implementing the very successful Genius Bar at Apple's retail stores. With much pomp and fanfare he arrived at JC Penney with the same mindset and culture that worked for him at Apple. He hired lieutenants from Apple with very generous compensation offerings, hoping to recreate the success at Apple stores. However, the approach that worked well at Apple ran counter to the needs of a very different customer at JC Penney. Many of the initiatives Johnson started floundered, sending JC Penney into a catastrophic downward spiral with all-time bad financials. In 2013, Johnson was fired from his post.

A related concept is the case where customer service varies across segments within the same business. Business owners need to be mindful of the many segments they serve and accordingly customize their services. Let me illustrate with an example. I am always meeting business partners over lunch sometimes at expensive restaurants, which advertise to business professionals. During these lunches, I expect to have a quiet lunch with little disturbance so that I can discuss some important topics with my business partners. However, it is quite common that during such lunches, a family with noisy kids is seated next to my table. The parents are constantly trying to manage the kids who are constantly trying to disturb everybody else around them. This is a classic example of a business attempting to satisfy two very different customer segments at once and failing at both—the poor parents feel bad as their kids are creating the disturbance and the business people feel frustrated for not being able to achieve their meeting objectives. In the end, both groups leave the restaurant unhappy and openly or subconsciously blame the establishment. It is important for the business owner to either focus on one segment (in fact, more and more restaurants are banning kids) or to compartmentalize more than one segment that they serve and ensure that everybody benefits from their best customer service.

Customer service is especially important to retail businesses because that is the only thing they have to offer to compete against online stores. Many retail stores are closing now, such as electronics stores, camera stores, book stores, even big department stores—because their customers can buy those same products more cheaply on the internet after they see and touch them in a store. It is more important than ever for businesses to analyze their customers and discover how they can make them happy—businesses must deeply understand their customer's experience.

CHAPTER 7

WHY SHOULD I INVEST IN EXPENSIVE COFFEMAKERS?

> *"Classic economic theory, based as it is on an inadequate theory of human motivation, could be revolutionized by accepting the reality of higher human needs, including the impulse to self-actualization and the love for the highest values."*
>
> ABRAHAM MASLOW

> *"The reptilian always wins. I don't care what you're going to tell me intellectually."*
>
> CLOTAIRE RAPAILLE

> *"It's getting cheaper and cheaper for users to innovate on their own. This is not traditional market research — asking customers what they want. This is identifying what your most advanced users are already doing and understanding what their innovations mean for the future of your business."*
>
> PROFESSOR ERIC VON HIPPEL, MIT

W HILE I HAVE VISITED OTHER branches of the Peninsula hotel group, the property in Shanghai has always stood out to me. The Peninsula Hotel on the Bund in Shanghai offers one of the most gratifying of customer experiences. Founded only recently in 2009, the Peninsula seamlessly blends the elegance and grandeur of the last century with the technology and comfort of this century. In 2013, it was voted the best Business Hotel in the world by the popular magazine, *Travel and Leisure*. The hotel went to great lengths to fine-tune every little detail a client would experience, consciously and subconsciously, from the moment you makes your booking to the moment you check out and even beyond. The hotel has designed every moment of the client's stay—in fact, "Peninsula Moments" is the motto of their marketing campaign.

Peninsula operates a customized fleet of vehicles to pick customers up from the airport. In fact, it is the only luxury hotel in Shanghai with a customized car fleet. The car fleet very much reflects the overall hotel experience: antique and modern, pomp and performance, fanfare and formality, solemnity and splendor, personal touch and global brands. The design of every detail—whether the upholstery of the car or the uniform of the driver—was done with thoughtfulness, care, compassion, and the end customer in mind. The design of the fleet is a function of art, science, and technology.

The hotel rooms at the Peninsula have been designed with utmost diligence. First, the lighting is perfect. The lamps are placed at the right spot around the room and provide ample light with a natural feel. The bedside lamps are lowered just right above the bedside tables. The lamps with the dresser provide the right amount of brightness and shadows, Hollywood-style, to allow a lady guest to get dressed, wear makeup, and look at herself in the mirror while feeling beautiful. The lampshades are translucent and provide the right luminance. The lighting around the room is controlled and adjusted via wall-panel touch and remote control technologies. Even with the lamps, the classical blends harmoniously with the modern. The décor of the lamps has a heritage feel and yet they make use of the latest control technologies.

The space in the suites has been designed to optimize best use. Walk-in closets, separate living rooms, large bathrooms with his and hers sinks, make-up areas with large mirrors, coffee-making corners with the latest coffee-making machines, private balconies and private pools are just a few features that make the hotel so luxurious. Beyond physical designs, the Peninsula has also removed all the frictions that irritate hotel guests. International long-distance calls and Wi-Fi are complementary. Deliveries to your room, like clean laundry, are made without disturbing the guests via wall-in boxes. One does not have to get out of the room (and get locked out naked in the hallway!) to pick up deliveries.

It is not that other hotels do not have these amenities but the Peninsula designed the whole environment with the customer in mind. Consider this: how many times do you make coffee using in-room coffeemakers at three-star hotels and motels? The coffee pots are usually stained, the coffee, cream, and sugar packs are usually old, and you are expected to use tap water to brew the drink. The end product is never tasty and hardly drinkable. Why then do these hotels bear the costs to add these cheap coffeemakers to their

LEE IHN (IKE)

rooms? The devices are either not used or leave the customer unsatisfied. They are added costs without a complementary increase in revenue in the form of repeat satisfied customers. The Shanghai Peninsula understood these details—upgrading the coffee-making experience through thoughtful design is a small price for the gain in satisfaction, confidence, trust, and loyalty of the customer.

Also, at any time, there is an elevator that is open and waiting for guests to walk in. This simple protocol anticipates the guests' arrival and provides a welcoming feel before they even enter their room. Guests do not wait for the elevator but rather the elevator waits for the guests! But beyond this, the hotel staff is always very courteous, very respectful, and very gentle.

Compare this to my experience at another high-end hotel, the Raffles Hotel in Cambodia, where I was nearly killed. The bathtubs in that hotel have a major design flaw—they have a curved base. Now, imagine an elderly person trying to step in or out of a wet bathtub with a curved base. It is a major slipping hazard! And that is exactly what happened to me—I slipped, almost fell, and hit my head against the ceramic sink! Hotels with these types of serious design flaws, if not addressed, could literally kill their customers and then kill their own businesses!

The aging Asian population

Across Asia, the population is fast aging. Birth rates have declined and life expectancy has increased, creating an imbalance in the young-to-old ratio in the populations of many countries, from

China to Japan to South Korea. This new reality poses some of the greatest challenges that these countries will face in the coming years. While there has been much press and talk about dealing with an aging population in Asia, many businesses seem to be ignoring this trend. Smart businesses should not only adjust to this new fact of life but rather should see this as an opportunity to develop new products to support the changing population.

Japan has more elderly citizens per capita than any other country in the world. As of September 2015, according to the Statistics Bureau with the Japanese Ministry of Internal Affairs and Communications, 26.7 percent of Japan's population are above sixty-five years of age, 12.9 percent are aged seventy-five or above and 4.0 percent are aged eighty-five or above. In 1989, only 11.6 percent of the population was aged sixty-five or above. That number is projected to rise to almost forty percent by 2055. Not only does Japan have the world's oldest people but the average age of the population is trending upwards very fast. As a result, the Japanese Health Ministry projects that the nation's total population will fall by twenty-five percent from 127.8 million in 2005 to 95.2 million by 2050.

South Korea is following Japan's footsteps. According to the Korea Statistical Office, the number of people aged sixty-five and above in South Korea stands at 11.7 percent of the country's population. Within fifteen years, this percentage will shift to close to twenty-five percent—one out of four South Koreans will be elderly. The reason for this dramatic shift in the Korean aging profile is two-fold: an increased life expectancy, which accompanied South Korea's economic growth, and a drop in women's fertility rate, which accompanied South Korea's post-war social revolution. Wonsik Choi, Senior Partner at McKinsey & Company in Seoul said, "The aging population is one of the most fundamental, structural shifts happening in Korea and affecting the growth prospects for the country. Just to give you an example, the working age population in Korea will peak at 37 million in 2016, and will diminish thereafter."

Any company doing business in Japan or South Korea needs to understand this dramatic paradigm shift in the profile of the customer base. Accordingly, products and services need to be retooled to accommodate this growing demographic. But, is that the case today? Are companies working towards improving products to meet the needs of the aging population?

My personal experience travelling to South Korea several times a year tells me otherwise. Simple common products are failing the elderly population in South Korea. Try twisting open soft drinks bottle caps, food jar caps, and even toothpaste caps as an elderly and you would quickly realize that you need Herculean force to achieve this feat. Forget about ripping open plastic packaging wraps, nylon packages, and other similar hard-to-open packages. The challenge is not limited to opening jars and packages—every product that requires force and strength is harder to use for the elderly, whether that product requires pulling a lever, lifting a weight, or moving a heavy object. There are so many easy and effective ways to make products and services friendly to the elderly. Print larger font manuals, keep your store wheelchair accessible, make signs bigger, etc.

By not paying attention to the needs of ten percent of the Korean customer base now, Korean companies are ignoring a tremendous potential growth opportunity as that piece of the pie gets bigger. There are a lot of rich people getting older! Since this problem is going to get worse as the population ages, these companies need to refocus their products to maximize their customer experience.

Deeper needs of the customer

Every customer pain point is an opportunity for a new, improved product or service. The more closely you can identify your customers' needs, the more successfully you can deliver the solution. And customer needs go beyond levers and packaging. Customers can easily compare product price points and features. We need to give customers a personal reason to choose us. What factors drive people to make these more intrinsic choices?

Imagine, for a minute, that you are at a restaurant seated at a table with a clean empty glass in front of you. You call the waiter and order a bottle of Perrier sparkling water. The waiter disappears for two minutes and returns with a cold bottle of the French beverage. Perrier water is sourced in Vergeze in Southern France and with its distinctive green bottle is symbolic of purity. In scenario A, you see that the waiter has already opened the bottle prior to returning to your table, approaches you and then proceeds to pour the water into the glass in front of you. In scenario B, the waiter brings an unopened Perrier bottle to your table, shows you the bottle, and you nod to him. Then he proceeds to open the bottle while you are watching and pours the sparkling water in the empty glass. Which scenario would you prefer?

Everybody I ask this question to always prefers scenario B. The question is why do we always prefer scenario B? The proximate answer is we feel more comfortable knowing that the water is coming from an unopened bottle. We do not have to consciously or unconsciously worry about the possibility, as remote as it is, that the waiter may have tampered with the beverage. The deeper answer is, as human beings, we choose situations, solutions, options, and products that satisfy our deep physiological, rational, emotional, and psychological needs and safety is just one such need. A product or a service designed to satisfy deep human needs will always be more appealing to customers. Knowing what these needs are gives you an advantage over others.

In 1943, American psychologist Abraham Maslow published a seminal paper titled "A Theory of Human Motivation" in the *Psychological Review*. In it he expounded his now famous theory that has come to be known as the hierarchy of needs. Maslow argued that human behavior is motivated by the satisfaction of certain needs in a very specific order. At our most basic level, we have certain physiological needs that have to be met. We all strive to meet those needs, or else our very own survival is at stake. These needs include air, water, and food to keep our body functioning; clothing and shelter to protect ourselves in our natural environment; and sexual activity for procreation and preservation of our species.

Once these basic physiological needs are generally met, the human person seeks to satisfy his or her safety needs. These include security of body, of employment, of resources, of morality, of the family, of health, and of property. In other words, we make sure that we are safe, our family is safe, we have good health, our homes are safe, our jobs are stable, and our properties are safeguarded.

The third level of human needs relate to love and belonging-ness. Once our survival needs are met and our safety is somewhat guaranteed, we seek friendship, companionship, and intimacy. These needs are inter-personal or social in nature. We become close to one person or a large group of persons to fulfill our needs to belong, to love and be loved.

The fourth level of needs is one that gives each one of us a sense of self-esteem and self-respect. Self-esteem includes the need for status, recognition, fame, prestige, and attention and self-respect includes the need for strength, competence, freedom, indepen-dence, and confidence. These needs are beyond economic—they achieve a sense of self-fulfillment that is very important to the indi-vidual. And lastly, at the highest level of needs the human being achieves what Maslow called self-actualization, when humans real-ize all their potential and becomes what they truly desire to be. This could be exploring creativity, spirituality or altruism towards others.

Maslow's theory of needs sheds light on how a human being has to fulfill their needs in a certain order as part of daily life. It is certainly not a new theory and it has not ceased from evolv-ing. The fourteenth century Andalusian scholar, Al-Shatibi, had identified several levels of human "necessities," namely preserva-tion of faith, of the soul, of wealth, of the mind, of offspring, and of honor that he believed were material to his society. Maslow himself revised his initial theory to later add two more level of needs—cognitive needs relating to knowledge, meaning, self-awareness, and aesthetic needs relating to beauty, balance, form. And more recently, Chilean economist Manfred Max Neef proposed a framework of human needs that are all inter-related. He identified the following needs: subsistence, protection, affection, understanding, participation, leisure, creation, identity, and freedom. The point I am making is this: it is important to understand what are the deep-rooted needs that motivate our customers and us. Designing businesses, products, and services that satisfy these needs will always win over competitors who fail to recognize such needs.

Clotaire Rapaille, founder of Archetype Discoveries Worldwide, has written several books claiming that buying decisions are made in the reptilian brain, the primitive part of the brain made up by the brain stem and the cerebellum. The human brain, according to a model proposed by American neuroscientist Paul MacLean and popularized by American cosmologist Carl Sagan, comprises of three parts: the rational part or the neo cortex where decisions are made using logic, the emotional part or the limbic system where emotions, memories, and habits reside, and the reptilian brain which reacts instinctively.

Rapaille argues that in most decision making the "reptilian always wins!" In other words, the average human person makes most decisions instinctively. Using this presumption, he has designed "regression sessions" where he taps into potential customers unconscious needs to discover their purchase preferences. As controversial as this approach is, Rapaille has been hired and has advised some of the largest companies on the planet—from P&G to Exxon to NASA. He helped design the PT Cruiser for

Chrysler by discovering what are the desired features of a car to meet the American psyche.

On more solid grounds, Daniel Kahneman, Nobel laureate, along with Amos Tversky developed a framework for explaining human behaviors where they postulated that the human mind operates on two levels: System One is fast, instinctive, and emotional whereas System Two is slower, deliberate, and logical.

I am not going to advocate for a method like Rapaille's but the lesson that I want to convey is the point I made above: understanding what motivates your customers consciously or unconsciously is a first important step to designing your products and services. Let us look at some examples.

The idea of safety, making the customer feel secure consciously or unconsciously using your product, is extremely important. In my travels across the world today, I still find transportation vehicles that make people feel very unsafe—whether it be an auto rickshaw in India that does not have a door securing the passengers inside or a bus in Thailand that is packed beyond capacity. These are usually simple design flaws and may not cost much to fix. But the designers or business managers fail to see that the fixes would unconsciously solve a basic human need—for which the customer may be willing to pay more.

On the other hand, I have also seen companies that go to great lengths emphasizing security. Several brands like Volvo and Michelin have made safety the very tag line by which they want their companies to be perceived in the public mindset. However, often some companies would take small unadvertised steps to make the customer feel secure. The doors in the Peninsula Hotel rooms are especially heavy. Holding them and opening them unconsciously give the guest a feeling of strength and solidness. This translates into a feeling of safety to be sleeping behind such doors.

Consider the need for self-respect. When we see mottos like "treat your customer like you would treat yourself" or "the customer is king," we are effectively catering to this basic human need. Treating a customer with respect, giving them the attention they deserve, listening to them when they speak and even when they complain is good for business not because they are trite behaviors that we do because management expects us to, but rather because they are what the customer expects deep inside. And satisfying this need earns you loyalty and trust.

Consider the need for a healthy, clean, and appealing environment. Many stores are crammed with products of all colors and sizes, stacked up high on unkempt shelves. The storekeeper believes that the more products he can display the more he will sell. But all he ends up achieving is an eyesore of a space. Unconsciously, he is turning off the customer the moment the customer walks into his store. The customer wants to run out of the store without even knowing why.

I experienced this in Korea. I once observed two stores side-by-side selling the exact same set of products. In one store, the clerks were at the door constantly calling passers-by in. They were loud to the point of being obnoxious. Once you walked into their store, they would pester you to the point of harassment. Products were everywhere and almost every item was labeled on "sale." In the second store, the clerks were well dressed and sat quietly at the back. They first engaged the customer with a smile and a welcome note. The items for sale were well arranged on visually appealing shelves and the clerks only took them off once the customer asked to see an item. Guess which store had more customers? The answer is obvious—the store that learned to appeal to the basic needs of the customer—needs of safety, security, personal space, and independence.

Along the same vein, simple clean designs like the Apple products are not only attractive to our eyes but are soothing to our deep human needs for beauty and aesthetics.

It usually takes a small effort to adjust our business, our processes, our policies, our products, and our services to ensure that we are meeting these deep customer needs. On the other hand, ignoring them could be very costly and goes against the grain of what we can provide to our customers. Too many companies do not pay enough attention to these needs and those who do always win.

Learn what the basic needs of your customer demographic are. Understand their motivations. Know whether they are spiritual or materialistic, liberal or conservative, introverts or extroverts, etc. and then design your products accordingly.

The axiom to rule them all

In my four decades of experience with businesses of all sizes and companies in many fields across the globe, I have come to believe that one single factor, when ignored, always causes the downfall of businesses: Customer Experience!

Customer Experience is the perspective-taking of the end-user of your business products and solutions. We have to see the world from the customer's point of view, to get in their minds, to empathize with their feelings, to feel their joy or pain, to walk in their moccasins. Customer Experience means we suspend our own judgment, overcome our own biases, avoid our own convictions, and favor those of the customer. Customer Experience means we design with the customer problem in mind, develop with the customer aesthetics in mind, sell with the customer end net value in mind.

I believe that feedback from customers, whether explicitly stated or implicitly implied, abounds around us. The customer is always giving us clues on what they want, what they are willing to pay a premium for and what will attract them to our businesses again. However, these clues are often hidden in our Blind Spot. We are so focused on the thousand activities that are required to run a business that it is easy to miss out on the most important factor that that will improve our Customer Experience and that will guarantee a return.

Libraries are filled with books on customer satisfaction. Terms such as "Voice of Customer," "Customer First," "Customer is King," and "Delighting Customers" are not only marketing bumper stickers but repeated business mantras. Corporations have whole departments now catering to the customer. We often hear of positions like "Chief Experience Officer" responsible for the overall "User Experience" and leading departments like "Customer Experience and Engagement." Certain companies such as P&G

and Amazon have retooled their whole cultures to improve customer satisfaction metrics.

Further, business schools offer whole courses on understanding and servicing customers. Behavioral economics foray into marketing aims to achieve just that goal. Phil Kotler, who is likely the most notable academician to study and advocate for the customer as the pinnacle of every business decision commented: "a highly satisfied customer generally stays loyal longer, buys more as the company introduces new products and upgrades existing products, talks favorably about the company and its product, pays less attention to competing brands, and is less sensitive to price, offers product or service ideas to the company, and costs less than new customers because transaction is routine."

At the same time, it is not always clear how small businesses and startups should look at Customer Experience. We are uncertain about how to satisfy a customer need when the customer is unaware of the need. Add to that the many skeptics of listening too closely to the customer. Steve Jobs, in an oft-quoted verse, said: "It's really hard to design products by focus groups. A lot of times, people don't know what they want until you show it to them." This is the case usually when a company is innovating in a totally new space. But what is the definition of Customer Experience for the small business, the sandwich shop or the street vendor?

I prescribe the use of Customer Experience not only as a pre-product design aid or post-launch refining mechanism but as a constant guide, like a lighthouse, that should direct every activity at every stage in a company's product lifecycles. Customer

Experience applies to all types and all sizes of companies as I've illustrated through many examples in my personal career. When we pay close attention to the customer needs, when we incorporate this information into the design of our products and services, and when we seek to increase the end net value to the customer, we can create a business that can potentially last forever!

CHAPTER 8

HOW DID THREE BOYS CREATE A $30 BILLION ECOSYSTEM?

"There is no passion to be found playing small—in settling for a life that is less than the one you are capable of living."
NELSON MANDELA

"Ignorance is the curse of God; knowledge is the wind wherewith we fly to heaven."
WILLIAM SHAKESPEARE

"Humility is the solid foundation of all virtues."
CONFUCIUS

ON A WARM DAY EARLY IN 1998, three young gentlemen walked into my office at the Lee Technology Consulting incubation center at the Stanford Research Park in Palo Alto, California. When Ken Xie, Feng Deng and Yan Ke came into my office that day and took a seat in front of me, I immediately could sense in them a level of passion mixed with deep technical knowledge and sincere humility. Within seconds of meeting them, in a true "blink" moment, I had already made up my mind that I would be investing in these young bright minds. That was no doubt one of the best investment decisions I would make over my career.

An idea and passion

Ken, Feng, and Yan hailed from China. They all graduated from the prestigious Tsinghua University and then attended top universities in the United States. Ken had earned an MS degree from Stanford. Feng received an MS degree from the University of Southern California and an MBA from the Wharton School. Yan received an MS degree from and completed his PhD at John Hopkins University. After graduating, they had worked at name-brand American technology companies—Intel, Cisco, Hughes, Healtheon, etc. Ken, Feng, and Yan were the types of top-level talent who were coming into the US from China in the early 1990s. They had impeccable academic credentials and were part of the pool of bright engineers powering Silicon Valley. Tsinghua University has been minting the brightest minds in technology for years now. The University prepares their students to have a global perspective and to be very practical—to be truly global citizens and successful engineers. Ken, Feng, and Yan exemplified this well-prepared Tsinghua graduate model in every sense of the word. Their technical knowledge was founded on solid grounds, was practical, and was comprehensive.

As my three guests explained their startup idea to me, two things became immediately clear. One, they had identified a real technological problem in a fast growing space and had conceived a genuine solution. Two, they were brimming with passion. Towards the end of the 1990s, the Internet was exploding. In 1995, only fourteen percent of American adults (ages eighteen plus) used the Internet to access information, whether to read their emails or browse web sites. By 1998, that percentage had more than doubled to thirty-six percent. By the end of the year 2000, fifty percent of American adults were online. As more people were getting online, it became clear that such growth could only be sustained if the whole system provided a level of security and trust that safeguarded its users' personal information and data.

Ken, Feng, and Yan had accurately predicted that a solid security solution, which did not undermine performance, would underpin the whole Internet ecosystem. They designed an ASIC-based Internet security system that acted as a high performance firewall. The hardware-based solution would not sacrifice the efficiency of the data traffic. As such it would be appealing to data centers and service providers. I immediately realized the market potential for such an innovation.

If the technical presentation of my three visitors gained my attention, it was their passion that gained my conviction. These three young men had the fire of entrepreneurship burning in their hearts. They were not satisfied with the status quo. They were not content with working from nine to five in a cubicle at a large corporation. They were not happy being followers. They desired to be masters of their own destiny. They wanted to become leaders. And, they were dreaming big!

Ken, Feng, and Yan came from humble origins. And when I came to know them, they retained that sincere sense of humility. While in my office, they would sit with their heads bowed down, would talk cautiously in a low voice, and would never interrupt. I took them out to lunch on several occasions and they would spend most of the time listening to me, smiling and being very polite. I visited their makeshift office in those days. The office was located in a nondescript part of town and was sparse with barely any furniture. Their initial lab consisted of computers resting on the floor. And yet these computers were running the software that would secure the growing Internet! Clearly, Ken, Feng, and Yan did not create an oversized image of themselves. They did not try to oversell themselves or their ideas. They were not flashy or arrogant. They were rather courteous, modest, and respectful.

These three criteria—passion, knowledge and humility—formed then and continue to form now the bedrock of Ken's, Feng's and Yan's personalities. They could not be failures and would not be failures. Within a week of meeting them, I signed them a check and invested in their company. That was, I believe, the fastest time from meeting a company's founders to me writing them a check. It was a personal record for me!

Over the next few months in this critical, initial phase of the company, I spent a lot of time advising the three founders and putting them in front of customers. I had numerous one-on-one meetings with Ken as he learned the ropes of the Chief Executive office. We looked at everything a startup needed—from operations to marketing to sales to corporate identity. I still recalled that they wanted to call the company "Eggies"! That would have been a very bad name for a company aiming to become a name brand in the global industry. After much debate and discussion, the name was changed and NetScreen was born! The new name had a melodious tune to it and succinctly described what the company was about—acting as a screen to Internet traffic. It is an example that I still use today to explain the importance of getting your corporate identity right from the beginning.

In its initial phase, a start-up is much like a racing car that has just taken off from the starting line. The pilot needs to apply his foot to the gas pedal as hard as he can and accelerate quickly to gain momentum. He needs to get any incremental advantage over the other cars. The race is very much ahead and the course is still very long to the finish line. But, a lack of focus and push at this crucial stage could be devastating to a fledgling company. It is usually at this stage that I spend a lot of time with promising start-ups. With NetScreen, I pushed on three main pedals to help accelerate the company: promotion, sales, and fundraising. I organized several events to help market the company. Ken and I were featured on a one-hour TV program in Korea explaining the company. I assisted the founders with selecting distributors in Korea and other places. I personally kept an eye on their sales and whether their sales targets were realistic and were being met. And, before Sequoia stepped in, I connected the founders with many potential investors in the Valley. All entrepreneurs need to keep pressure on these three gas pedals in the early phase of their companies: promotion gets the word out, sales gets revenues in, and fundraising ensures growth.

I often discussed with the NetScreen founders the value of what they were building to the customer. As technical as an Internet firewall product is, it is still extremely important to design and build it with the end customer in mind. In the early days of the company, we were getting overwhelmed with complaints about technical issues and software bugs after deployment and on premises. These early challenges are an important reminder that the customer is especially important when a company is trying to gain momentum and traction.

So, we interpreted the meaning of customer experience in light of such a technical product. We asked ourselves the question as to what problems were frustrating the customers most. And how would our solutions remove those frustrations? I pushed for more testing prior to shipping the product out. We debated whether customers would see value in the offering right away or whether they needed to be convinced. We questioned whether the product was simple enough, appealing enough, robust enough, and efficient enough to really delight the customer. Through these growing pains, we improved the product significantly and delivered a winning solution for our customers and our investors.

Soon, NetScreen was gaining attention and was making a name for itself. The company started attracting the marquis investors in the Valley. Sequoia poured in capital and reinforced the management team, bringing in Robert Thomas as CEO and replacing Ken. The company was growing rapidly by the time Y2K arrived. But, these were not smooth times. In late 1990s the dotcom bubble in Silicon Valley started seeing cracks and would soon be bursting. The environment was very tough and the whole technology industry was being rattled. Founders were going bankrupt, engineers were losing their jobs, and investors were losing trust. The NetScreen racing car had to speed ahead in a stormy weather— the winds were blowing weaker cars off the track and the rain and lack of visibility had many founders crash into each other.

However, NetScreen was being managed differently. Its pilots' passion, knowledge, and humility would see them through all of these challenges. With a solid hardware-based solution in a growing space and with a brand that was being recognized worldwide, NetScreen was poised to stay on track. With a focus on customer satisfaction, i.e., the finish line, NetScreen was delighting its customers and they were booking orders rapidly. Its competitors' software-only solution did not achieve the same level of performance technically and had nowhere the same brand prestige. NetScreen would come out of the tech bubble burst unscathed.

In December 2001, only three months after the tragic events of 9/11 in New York City, NetScreen went public. That was not a very logical time to go public. The country was still recovering from the terrorist attacks, unprecedented in US history. There was a lot of uncertainty about the future. Everybody was worried about other possible attacks, sleeper cells, personal safety, and how America would respond militarily. War was definitely on the horizon. But, how would the economy fare? Would public investors trust the market again?

In this difficult environment, the NetScreen founders and advisors decided to go public. They were very aware of the challenging times but they also knew that their company and solutions would give hope to a market that was barely recovering. On its opening day, NetScreen stocks surged forty-eight percent! Even though the company had not made a profit at the time, it sold 10 million shares at $16 per share before opening through its lead underwriter, Goldman Sachs. The public investors responded very warmly to NetScreen. They were ready to be hopeful again—to put their trust in technological marvels, sound leadership, and a bright vision. And they rewarded NetScreen. By 2004, NetScreen was dominating the Internet security space. And, that year Juniper Networks acquired NetScreen for $4 billion.

<u>Wonder in the Valley</u>

Throughout this incredible journey—from young humble friends in my office to Silicon Valley billionaires, Ken, Feng, and Yan continued to hold as vital the potion of success—passion plus knowledge plus humility. First, when Sequoia brought in a new CEO, Ken left NetScreen and after some time off formed another company called Fortinet. In 2000, I relocated to the beautiful Pacific

Northwest. Ken and his brother Michael visited me at my residence in North Seattle that year and pitched their new company to me. I knew that investing in Ken would be a safe and rewarding bet. So, I came in as an early investor in Fortinet and as an advisor to Ken. As with NetScreen, I helped Ken promote the company in Korea and introduced him to customers. We hired a country manager that would push sales in the region. I often made the trip to the newly opened Fortinet R&D branch in Vancouver to oversee the hiring of engineers and management practices. I once again mentored Ken on the importance of corporate identity and encouraged him when he considered changing the name from ApSecure to Fortinet—a nice blend of the words "fort" and ""internet." Ken would lead Fortinet to great success. The company was recognized in *Forbes Magazine, Entrepreneur Magazine* and on the Deloitte Fast 500 list. In 2009, the company filed for its initial public offering, opening at $12.50 per share and closing the same day at $16.62, a thirty-three percent increase. In August 4 of 2015, Fortinet's market cap peaked at $8.36 billion!

NetScreen's and Fortinet's success has since spread far and wide. The founders have acted as role models for many other success stories both in America and in Asia. Some of the companies' top executives went on to form or lead their own great companies. Nir Zuk, who came to NetScreen through the acquisition of OneSecure, founded Palo Alto Networks. Robert Thomas, who was the CEO of NetScreen, later became the CEO of Infoblox. Palo Alto Networks market cap peaked at $16.5B in 2015 and Infoblox market cap peaked at $2.5B in 2013. By my count, NetScreen and Fortinet have in some way or another assisted in establishing a

$30 billion ecosystem. Further, these two companies were pioneering examples proving that companies launched and managed by Asian talent could become blockbusters. They effectively established Asian engineers as very capable entrepreneurs. Not only did the achievements of Ken, Feng, and Yan garner the respect of investors and customers worldwide, they became role models to countless would-be entrepreneurs. The fire of entrepreneurship, lighted by people like Ken, Feng, and Yan, is now burning strongly in the hearts of many Chinese entrepreneurs. Currently 3.6 million start-ups are being founded every year in China. The Chinese entrepreneurship machine is well and strong, producing some of the finest companies the world has seen. Companies like Baidu, Alibaba, and Tencent are a testament to that fact.

I have continued a long friendship with Ken to this date. We meet often over good Korean food or over a game of golf when I am in the Valley. I like to joke with Ken that the only change I see in him after all these years and two blockbuster successes is his hair that has turned gray. Ken remains the polite, humble, and gracious person who walked into my office twenty years ago. Passion, knowledge, and humility still form the bedrock of his personality.

After holding very senior positions at Juniper Networks, Feng and Yan decided to return to China and launched Northern Light Venture Capital in 2005. The investment firm was well positioned to benefit from the growing Chinese economy and from the large entrepreneur spirit developing in China in the 2000s. To-date Northern Light has $1.7 billion in committed capital from leading global investors and has backed over one hundred companies. Feng now serves on the Board of Directors of the Tsinghua

University Foundation and is a member of several other non-profit advisory boards, including the Stanford Institute for Economic Policy Research. I even heard that he has overcome his shyness and gives lectures across the country these days!

Before leaving the US for China in 2005, Feng reached out to me. He sent me this very kind email and told me that he was repatriating to the motherland and was very appreciative of the time we spent together in the early days of NetScreen. Once more, I was touched by the display of humility. It is these enduring characteristics and values that mark a true leader. I told Feng that I learned as much from him as he from me. I tremendously enjoyed his friendship.

These three gentlemen have become an important part of my own journey. I often wonder how far my journey with them took me and I wonder how far it can still take me. I have met many impressive people over my career and I continue to meet promising entrepreneurs daily. I am in some way on a constant quest to discover and assist more friends like Ken, Feng, and Yan. And I know I have found them when I see the combination of passion, knowledge, and humility in their characters.

CHAPTER 9

IS MY COMPANY READY FOR PRIMETIME?

"Don't start a business. Find a problem. Solve a problem. The business comes second."
ROBERT HERJAVEC, SHARK

"A complainer is like a Death Eater because there's a suction of negative energy. You can catch a great attitude from great people."
BARBARA CORCORAN, SHARK

"I am not shy in asking for help. I know what I don't know and don't pretend otherwise. This has served me well both as a student when I was younger and as an adult in my professional life. I have always believed that asking questions from experts and seeking out help is a sign of strength, not weakness."
TALIA GOLDFARB, SHARK TANK WINNER

*"Innovation distinguishes between
a leader and a follower."*
STEVE JOBS

"There's a way to do it better—find it."
THOMAS EDISON

M ANY BUDDING ENTREPRENEURS visited my incubation center at the Stanford Research Park in Palo Alto, California over the 1990s and early 2000s—from fresh college graduates dressed in jeans who were convinced that they would become the next Bill Gates to formally dressed technology industry veterans who were tired of working decades in the corporate world and wanted to try their luck at building their own companies. Many of them fit one profile or another and it took painstaking, long meetings to sift the true winners from those who were simply there to waste my time and their time.

I am often asked by students what makes an entrepreneur stand out while giving a pitch? Or how do entrepreneurs know when they are ready to launch their business? How do they know when their idea is fully developed? What is the likelihood they will succeed? Do I think their company will make it?

My answer is how many hard questions have you asked yourself?

Shark Tank

Over seven million Americans tune in to their TVs every week to watch a reality show called Shark Tank. Shark Tank features real-life investors sitting comfortably on a panel and vetting business ideas from entrepreneurs. The entrepreneurs are selected from thousands of applicants who want to be on the TV show and who are looking for money, publicity, and connections to grow their businesses. The investors, known as the Sharks, are well-known and successful entrepreneurs. The format of the show follows a typical entrepreneur/investor pitch, where the entrepreneur stands in front of the Sharks, explain the business, and ask the Sharks for money in exchange for equity in the company. The Sharks in turn quiz the entrepreneur, vet the idea, discuss and debate openly among themselves, and then decide if they each want to invest in the entrepreneur's company. They negotiate general terms with the entrepreneur live and if one or more Sharks choose to invest, they invest their personal money in the pitched business.

The show has garnered much popularity since its inception in 2009. It has also collected several TV awards. Viewership and its primetime TV ranking have both been increasing over the past few years. Further, spin-offs of the show are expected to air in other countries, including in Portugal, Australia, and Italy.

The popularity of the show can be attributed to the frank, often entertaining, exchange between the Sharks and the entrepreneurs and also to the dynamics of the exchange among the Sharks themselves. The entrepreneur's business idea is decomposed and debated. Their assumptions are cross-examined. The whole experience forces the entrepreneur to get to the business' basic core and revisit the presumptions of the business model. If these hold, they will secure an investment. If not, they will go home empty handed. A good analogy of the whole process is as if the entrepreneur has stitched together a woolen sweater. The Sharks will pull at any tread that is exposed. If the pull causes the sweater to start unraveling, the whole business model will collapse. But, if the pull confirms that the knots are secure, then the model stays in place and secures an investment.

I really love the show for many reasons. I particularly love the show for the frank and honest discussion that enables a business idea to be scrutinized. I think that such a vetting process of any business idea ought to be part of every business practice. Let us take a look at some key questions we can ask ourselves based on the Shark Tank model.

DO I SEEK OUT AND LISTEN TO DIALOGUE?

The pitch on Shark Tank is an exercise where investors and entre- preneurs are brought together to carry an open and purpose- driven dialogue. It is a free exchange of perspectives on a common idea or business proposal. You should encourage open dialogues in all departments of your company. Create environments to get employees and management talking. Many companies, especially in the high technology sector, have removed wall offices in favor of open working spaces to encourage such mixing of people and mixing of ideas. Take concrete steps to nurture an environment where people increase their opportunities to meet and discuss. Do not formalize meetings but encourage frequent, short, ad-hoc opportunities for people to talk to each other candidly. These could be encouraging lunch in the company cafeteria by offering free food, like what Google does, or calling for daily standing or check-in meetings, like what the Agile process calls for.

HOW CAN I AVOID GROUPTHINK?

Encouraging open dialogues, however, is not enough. You need to ensure that the group does not get trapped into biases that cause them to all reinforce the same idea. On Shark Tank, the Sharks are continuously challenging and competing with each other. Enable an atmosphere where it is healthy for participants to push others' assumptions, theories, proposals, and perspectives. Encourage constructive criticisms of every idea. Vet every proposal from various angles. Leave no rock unturned. You can ensure that this happens by appointing formal roles in every meeting. Appoint one person to be the challenger. And train your leaders so that they ask the right questions to challenge their teams' perspectives. Several management techniques, such as Precision Questioning, teach leaders how to do just that.

HOW CLEARLY DO I COMMUNICATE?

Co-founder of Intel, Andy Grove said, "How well we communicate is determined not by how well we say things but how well we are understood." Effective communication is extremely important. In the Shark Tank sessions, as in all Venture Capital sessions, entrepreneurs have a narrow few minutes to make the case for their business. During that time, every second is precious. What you say is as important as what you do not say. And how you say it is as important as when and why you said it. How you are perceived and understood in these brief moments may well decide your whole future. It is not possible to overemphasize the importance of clear, concise, and impactful communication in business as well as in our general life. The problem is that effective communication abilities do not come naturally to most of us. As a company owner and a leader, it is your responsibility to develop the right set of training sessions to help your employees communicate better. These training sessions need to be repeated and preferably repeated often.

DO I SHARE AND RECEIVE FEEDBACK TRUTHFULLY?

But the ability to communicate effectively is not enough. A con man is a master communicator. You need to establish a set of values that directs a company to take a truthful and pragmatic view of any problem. This is easier said than done. Many cultures encourage what I call "micro-lying." This is a habit where we tell small lies consciously or unconsciously. We avoid telling the whole truth for some other perceived higher reason. This reason could be cultural, where a junior employee views speaking openly to a superior as a sign of disrespect. The reason could be traditional, where the larger group has a habit of polishing over facts or sweeping issues under the rug. Or it could be due to momentum: everybody is doing it, so why should I be the exception? In any case, these reasons to avoid digging deep into an issue and uncovering all sides rationally are very costly. In Shark Tank, I am amazed by the frankness of some of the Sharks. They do not mince words. They say it like they see it. They un-turn every rock. They look at all angles. They ask many questions. They are not scared of asking what they do not understand. They are not worried about what others think about them. This level of probing requires confidence and confidence is stronger than mere appearance. Any business that is serious about winning the Sharks over needs to develop this sense of frankness and confidence in their employees. Micro-lying is bad. Drop it, adopt frankness, and you will see miracles happen.

DO I SEEK OUT DIFFERENT OPINIONS?

The Sharks come from very different backgrounds. Mark Cuban grew up in Pittsburg, attended Kelley School of Business, made his initial fortune in software, and now owns the Dallas Mavericks and a chain of movie theatres. Robert Herjavec was born in Croatia, grew up in Canada, attended the University of Toronto, and was a stay-at-home dad before launching an IT security company. Lori Greiner grew up in Chicago, the second daughter of a real estate agent and a psychologist, attended Loyola University, owns 120 patents, invented a jewelry box that made her rich, and is known as the "Queen of QVC" for the shopping network.

Diversity adds strength to a team. It allows different team members to look at the same problem from different points of view. It is a sure way to challenge the groupthink problem discussed above. It forces a problem to be analyzed using various techniques—team member using their own techniques that worked for them in the past. Ensure you build diversity of backgrounds, cultures, experiences, education, and opinions when you hire or when you build a team.

DID I FORGET THE FUNDAMENTALS?

Always question the basics of any business plan. Many people get enamored with complexity. They love to discuss grand plans and audacious goals. Every now and then you meet someone who believes they can solve the Earth's problems. But a solid business does not stand on complexity. Rather it stands on sound fundamentals. The Sharks are really good at uncovering whether the basics of the business being pitched are solid or not. They ask simple questions: what is your economic viability, how much debt do you have, who are your partners, what previous experiences have you had, etc. In your organization too, train your leaders to always question the basics. Test the elemental economic theories. Question the simple engineering. Vet the core legal principles.

AM I COURTEOUS WHILE I DISAGREE?

To really enable a team to engage in serious and constructive discussions, without creating inter-personnel problems, you need to manage the team members' behaviors. When challenged, we all get defensive and our defensive mechanisms include everything from refusing to give up our position on a situation even when proven wrong to getting physical with the opposing party. Emotions run high, tempers are raised, voices get louder, and soon you have a shouting match. It is important that people realize that the discussion and debate is on the ideas and not themselves. This is easier said than done. The Sharks can get very critical of each other but they never lose respect for each other.

You need to establish an environment where your employees feel encouraged to challenge each other's ideas but remain steadfastly courteous in doing so and never criticize each other's person. Establish rules for objective discussions. Never allow the discussion to get personal. Correct immediately and severely if and when boundaries are crossed.

DO I SHARE REWARDS ALONG WITH RESPONSIBILITIES?

The Sharks invest their own money into the entrepreneurs' companies. They do not invest the network's money. And in return, they benefit from the success of the investment as they take equity in these companies. They have the greatest incentive to ensure that their investment succeeds. Hence, the discussion with the entrepreneur is extremely important to them personally.

It is important that every company creates a sense of responsibility as well as an opportunity for reward for employees based on decisions they make. Make sure your employees have skin in the game. This can be done by increasing your profit-sharing plan, calculating bonuses based on the return of the company, or rewarding employees regularly with small tokens of appreciation.

DO I ALWAYS TRUST THE MAJORITY?

It is quite rare to have a situation where all Sharks together invest in a company. It is also certainly not common to have a majority of Sharks invest in the same company. In other words, you do not need a situation where a majority of Sharks need to be right for a company to be a deemed a worthy investment.

While majority rules is a fair and satisfying method to select an option among many, as in selecting a political candidate, it is not necessarily a preferred method at arriving at sound business decisions. Many times a problem can be so challenging that the majority of people looking at the problem will propose the wrong solution. It is important for you to recognize the expert, the long-term focuser, the systems thinker, the leader, the visionary in your team and give their opinion more weight than others.

DO I STOP PAYING ATTENTION TOO SOON?

While the Shark Tank show usually ends with a smiling entrepreneur who has secured funding, the Sharks involvement does not end there. In fact, many "winner" entrepreneurs end up not getting financed because the on-air offers are contingent upon further diligence and they fail such diligence. And the Sharks remain involved in monitoring the companies long after they are funded.

Once a decision has been made, keep the door open to follow up on whether actions are being implemented to fulfill the decision and follow through to see the end result. Keep options alive to revisit the decision once more data becomes available or if the situation changes. Remain dynamic and remain persistent. Very few wins are hole-in-one shots.

What do companies in Silicon Valley know?

Silicon Valley, the area between San Jose and San Francisco and home to many high-tech companies, employs over 1.5 million people. Between 2007 and 2014, the United States' economy created only an additional 0.4 job per one hundred whereas San Francisco County alone added 13.1 jobs in the same time period. Per capita income and the Value Added per employee (gross domestic product divided by total employment) is significantly higher for Silicon Valley compared to the rest of the United States. And, Silicon Valley accounts for a large percentage of all patents registered in the United States. By all measures, Silicon Valley has managed to establish an economy that is unsurpassed by any other geographical region or city not only in the United States but in the rest of the world. The question then is: what is it that is so different in Silicon Valley?

I think the best answer to this question has been given by MIT Professor Timothy J Sturgeon in the book *Understanding Silicon*

Valley by Martin Kenney. Professor Sturgeon notes: "Perhaps the strongest thread that runs through the Valley's past and present is the drive to 'play' with novel technology, which, when bolstered by an advanced engineering degree and channeled by astute management, has done much to create the industrial powerhouse we see in the Valley today." In other words, a culture of innovation deeply rooted in science and engineering encouraged and managed by smart leaders is what led to the unique and phenomenal growth of Silicon Valley.

Over the past decade, innovation has become a quick mantra on the lips of many. Volumes of books have been written on this topic alone. Corporate readers repeat the buzzword almost like an incantation without truly understanding what it means. In fact, few companies implement tangible steps to move their products, processes, manufacturing, marketing, and sales from an always-done-that-way to novel-ways-that-challenge-the-status-quo mode. Innovation requires proactive effort by the leadership, participation of everybody in the company, and a tolerance of risk by the stakeholders.

In short, innovation requires the establishment and nurture of a certain culture within every company. How do we know if a company is building the right culture to sustain success?

DOES LEADERSHIP INVEST IN NEW IDEAS?

Innovation cannot be delegated. Innovation is the CEO's responsibility and priority. Since innovation is the only element that allows a company to look forward and prevents it from remaining stagnant, it is the leader's responsibility to ensure that it is given proper attention. The CEO needs to push innovation that is aligned with the company's vision, communicate its importance to the employees, make budget available so that it is encouraged, and appoint other leaders to be responsible to see its implementation. The CEO needs to be held accountable to oversee that a culture of innovation permeates the company.

DO WE SUPPORT IDEAS THAT COME FROM ANYONE AND ANYWHERE?

Everybody at every level of the company needs to take part in the innovation process. This means that everybody in the company, from the night shift janitor to the executive vice president, needs to be constantly thinking about what can be done to improve the company. There are many reasons why every employee needs to be made responsible for innovation. Each employee sees the company from a different perspective and they bring their own backgrounds and experiences in perceiving solutions to problems and inefficiencies. Tapping into that collective brainpower and expecting the solution to come from anybody is the only way a company should approach innovation.

And innovation should not happen only at special meetings called by management. Dedicated brainstorming sessions are a great way to encourage and collect ideas from employees. But a true culture of innovation encourages employees to innovate all the time and everywhere. Steve Jobs once said "But innovation comes from people meeting up in the hallways or calling each other at 10:30 at night with a new idea, or because they realized something that shoots holes in how we've been thinking about a problem." In fact, many innovations happen accidentally without planning, at no set time and no set place. The ubiquitous Post-It was invented by accident— an engineer at 3M created a weak adhesive while trying to create a strong adhesive and another engineer later attempted to use the adhesive to keep markers in a hymn book that he uses to sing in a church choir! These two events were completely accidental and came together fortuitously to bring us the now universal note taker!

DO WE CONSIDER ALL AREAS OPEN TO IMPROVEMENT?

We often times confuse innovation with improvement in products only. While product innovation is critically important, innovation should happen in everything a company does. We need to think of innovation in the broadest terms. A company can innovate everything—from processes to manufacturing to the way it documents strategies to tools it uses to manage its operations to HR policies. In other words, innovation is an improvement on everything a company does that results in better products, cheaper costs, faster time to market, more satisfied customers, and a sharper competitive edge.

ARE WE INVESTING IN IDEAS THAT SOLVE REAL PROBLEMS?

Innovation does not result in solutions that are interesting theoretically without a customer to ultimately use it. Innovation is rooted in reality and not in fiction. Many concept products are very appealing from an engineering point of view but can never succeed in the market. This could be because the engineering will not work efficiently, or the product is not viable from a cost point of view or it would hardly solve a customer problem. Remember the old adage about the king who wanted to build a castle in the air—an interesting idea that is bound to fail and has little value. Your innovation process should not be geared to produce castle-in-the-air ideas. Rather, innovation needs to be carried out with the customer always in mind. A market must exist to ultimately consume what is being developed and profit needs to be generated from such a product and market.

ARE YOU IGNORING YOUR GUT?

Innovation is triggered by feedback from the customer and end user. That feedback can be gathered in many ways—from focus groups to analyzing customer complaints to silently observing customer behaviors. But, innovation is also triggered by sheer gut feelings of employees within the company. Innovation requires seeing what the customers and what others may not be able to see. Compromising on the average in this case only results in average products.

A good example of this customer feedback-gut feeling nexus is the introduction of the large screen by Samsung on their smart phones. There was a time when all innovation in the cell-phone industry centered on miniaturization. Yet Samsung took a counter-vailing approach and introduced some phone models with large size. And soon the large screen was key to ushering in mobile commerce. It enabled people to more comfortably transact via their mobile devices. Here, Samsung noted an industry trend and then trusted their gut feelings in trying a risky design and changed the industry.

ARE YOU INVESTING REAL RESOURCES IN NEW IDEAS?

While the action of innovation itself needs to be freewheeling, i.e., employees need to be free to think outside of the box and not be restrained in voicing their ideas, the process to encourage innovation in a company needs to be well defined. A company needs to establish processes and policies to encourage innovation. It should provide guidelines to ensure employees are dedicating part of their time reflecting on the next big thing. Google famously had implemented the twenty-percent policy where employees can work on whichever project they choose for twenty percent of their work time. Further, a company needs to implement tools in place to solicit ideas, filter through them, rank the ideas, and push good ideas to implementation.

HAVE WE TESTED OUR IDEAS?

"Eat your own dog food" is a colloquialism that originated at Microsoft in the 1980s to mean employees should try their own products first. The term has since been broadly adopted in the technology industry and used as a mantra to push employees to test their own ideas and products before releasing them to the customer. This not only enables employees to see the idea in action and find its faults, weaknesses, and strengths but also allows them to build confidence in the products.

DO WE ACCEPT FAILURE?

The process of innovation, by definition, is bound to be a process full of failures. When we try something new, it is not always possible to see all the ways the idea can work and similarly all the ways it cannot work. It is important to allow failures because that is the only way we can surface how the product will not fail. Thomas Edison was known to have said, "I have not failed, not once. I've discovered ten thousand ways that don't work." Hence, never reprimand employees for ideas that do not work. Instead, reward them for ideas that truly work. Acknowledge them in front of others with visible awards. And give them monetary incentive, preferably tied to the monetization of the successful idea.

DO WE KEEP OUR METRICS FLEXIBLE?

While setting goals and objectives to be met during a process of innovation, avoid measuring whether your innovation culture is successful by traditional corporate metrics, like number of ideas generated, return per idea, or average cost per idea. Good ideas follow a power law distribution, which means a few good ideas will generate most of the return to your company and the vast majority of ideas will generate little or no return. Hence, chase these few ideas and avoid measuring the efficiency or success of your process using averages and short-term metrics.

Richard Branson, chairman of the Virgin Group, said, "There is no substitute for innovation. Original ideas will always rise to the top." However, innovation does not happen in a vacuum. Smart innovative companies take the lead and establish a strong culture of innovation. And those who do, change the world!

CHAPTER 10

DO I EVEN KNOW WHAT I DON'T KNOW?

"I have a dream that my four little children will one day live in a nation where they will not be judged by the color of their skin but by the content of their character."
MARTIN L. KING, JR.

" "There's actually a bunch of psychology theory that even making small decisions around what you wear or what you eat for breakfast, things like that, they kind of make you tired and consume your energy."
MARK ZUCKERBERG, WHEN ASKED ABOUT WHY HE WEARS THE SAME GRAY SHIRT ALL THE TIME

"Quality is not an act, it is a habit"
ARISTOTLE

*"If you are going to achieve excellence in big things,
you develop the habit in little matters. Excellence is
not an exception, it is a prevailing attitude."*

COLIN POWELL

*"If you are born poor it's not your mistake,
But if you die poor it's your mistake."*

BILL GATES

FTER LEAVING DAEGU FOR the United States, I had to learn many lessons along to way to becoming who I am today. Some of these lessons were painful or embarrassing, but I will share them with you. Most importantly, I learned chemistry applies to everything in life. Whether I can impress investors, connect to an audience, or get an interview always involves my ability to connect with the other people in the room on a personal level.

Many years ago when I was a young man, I was presenting an important project to an American audience in a quiet conference room. The conference was arranged during lunch time and we had sandwiches catered in. Afterwards, I felt very confident the presentation had gone well. So I was dumbfounded to get the bad news that the committee did not pick my project. Later, I asked an American colleague at the company what he thought had gone wrong.

My American friend was kind enough to give me some advice: chew your sandwiches more quietly! It is perfectly normal in Asian culture to eat loudly, and I was hardly thinking about the noise I was making while eating because I was so focused on my presentation.

Could my loud chewing and poor table manners have distracted and turned off the committee and actually have impacted the outcome of my business deal? I started to compare the eating habits of my Asian and American friends and began to wonder if he was right.

Montesquieu in 1769 said, "commerce polishes and softens barbarian ways as we can see every day." The Scottish historian William Robertson, a contemporary of Adam Smith's, refined this statement further to "commerce softens and polishes the manners as early as 1704, Samuel Ricard wrote: "commerce haracter which distinguishes it from all other professions. It affects the feelings of men so strongly that it makes him who was proud and haughty suddenly turn supple, bending and serviceable. Through commerce, man learns to deliberate, to be honest, to acquire manners, to be prudent and reserved in both talk and action. Sensing the necessity to be wise and honest in order to succeed, he flees vice, or at least his demeanor exhibits decency and seriousness so as not to arouse any adverse judgment on the part of present and future acquaintances."

This theory of gentle commerce ("doux commerce") posits that man develops kindness and good manners when transacting with each other. The economist Herb Gintis noted "societies that use markets extensively develop a culture of cooperation, fairness and respect for the individual." Thomas Friedman, in his book *The World is Flat* talks about the "Double Arch Theory", i.e., nations that operate McDonald's stores, in effect, nations open to trade, do not go to war. It is, in fact, in a businessperson's best interests to be kind and gentle to ensure customers are best served.

Survival lessons from the business world

Throughout my career working in the defense electronics and telecommunications industry, as a Venture Capitalist leading multiple IPOs and nearly a hundred M&As, as an advisor and consultant to numerous startups and large corporations, and as a philanthropist, I have learned to be very mindful of my personal habits that might negatively reflect upon me and impact my success. And I try to share these lessons with my students so they can avoid losing a business deal over a tuna sandwich! I've had more than one student contact me years later and thank me for helping them look good.

How much do my manners really matter?

Acting appropriately in the presence of others is more than a sign of respect and decorum. Rather, good manners send a signal that put others around you at ease and in a positive, welcoming mood. Good manners show others that you respect and value them. Good manners set the environment for others to be convivial towards you. They remove distraction and encourage friendliness, cordiality, and cooperation. In a business setting, if you are subconsciously irritating a customer in your presence because of your bad manners, you have lost the business. Good manners towards your customer are the foundation of good customer experience!

I have stopped making loud noises when I eat, making noises with my knife and fork, ignoring others when they are talking, talking over others, interrupting them in the middle of a conversation, raising my voice unnecessarily and cutting waiting lines.

I have adopted checking my table manners, eating graciously, being cognizant of others, listening attentively, nodding when others speak, speaking softly, using the words "please" and "thank you" and following the rules.

Shouldn't my product matter more than my smile?

Dr. Albert Mehrabian, author of *Silent Messages*, found that over 90% of all daily communication is non-verbal. The American poet William Arthur Ward noted, "A warm smile is the universal language of kindness." A smile is effectively a substantial part of your exchange with a customer—its impact on your customer is likely larger than the words that you say. Further, smiling is infectious. Exchanging smiles are the first step to agreeing to cooperate and the first step towards a business deal.

I have stopped looking glum and austere, appearing serious all the time, and associating a somber expression with thoughtfulness, associating sadness and tears with compassion.

I have adopted smiling all the time and to everybody, having a gracious and amicable look, appearing confident, associating a happy expression with caring and genuineness.

Should I keep a serious business demeanor to show my commitment and competence?

"Laughter is the best medicine" goes the old adage. I believe that laughter not only cures what is broken but prevents the ailments in the first place. Laughter melts hearts, thaws frozen relationships, chases fears, buries jealousy, and brings out compassion, kindness, and joy. My good friends and neighbors Karen and Bill Stuht are a lovely couple who have been happily married for sixty-two years! When a local magazine asked them for the secret to their long and happy relationship, Karen advised, "If you expect to last sixty-two years, you better have a sense of humor." Karen's advice should be heeded not only by couples but also by business people alike!

I have stopped believing that the boss needs to be serious, associating anger with authority, or associating bantering with disrespect.

I have adopted believing that the boss needs to be an approachable friend, associating laughter with consideration and esteem, and starting my conversation with a polite, funny and appreciative comment.

When should I give my opinion?

The elders in Africa have a good saying: "until the lion tells his own story, the hunter will always be the hero!" In other words, you have to tell your side of your story. We are ultimately responsible for our own image. Nobody is as efficient an advocate for us as our own selves. We know our own selves best. Grabbing the bull by the horns and taking charge of how others view us is not being arrogant but rather it is being responsible. We need to place the burden of how we ought to be seen directly on our own shoulders and we should not rely on others to tell or get our story right.

I have stopped waiting for others to speak on my behalf, relying on others to make my case, avoiding voicing my opinions even when I am in doubt, or associating quietness with humility.

I have adopted speaking first for myself, not fearing my own ideas, not fearing being rejected, not fearing being wrong, taking charge of my own message, taking responsibility for my own words and associating expressiveness with confidence.

Everyone exaggerates, right?

We all tell small lies, also known as white lies. Dan Ariely, Professor of Behavioral Economics at Duke University, has shown that we all cheat a little and the reasons for doing so are often complex. We may tell white lies due to behavioral biases or our need to rationalize certain situations. However, when the small lies manifest into habits that impact our lives and others' lives, we are treading on a path towards dishonesty and loss. It is our duty to be aware of untruths that we tell to get a short-term advantage over others and to rout these out of our lives for a more permanent gainful association with those whom we deal with.

I have stopped saying that "I am on my way!" when I have not even started, overstating my position to appear important and savvy, or overcommitting my word to get a deal done.

I have adopted saying only what I mean, ensuring that my statements are accurate and truthful, and standing by promises I make however small they are.

Is networking the most important use of my free time?

In the past decade or so, a lot of research has been conducted on human networks and their importance to businesses. Companies like

LinkedIn shot up in valuation capitalizing on this basic need for people to grow and maintain a business network. The overarching and implicit reason for maintaining such a network is that at one point you can tap into the network with a personal request and for a personal benefit. All of that is good but what bothers me is many times people tend to believe that substituting the network for personal talent, skills, education, and experience will get them ahead. Relying solely on your network, such as your school network, without placing emphasis on your underlying abilities is a recipe for collective disaster. It discourages excellence, borders on patronage and clientelism, and hints at corruption. Build your talent and skills to get ahead first, then amplify these with your network. Elevate what you know to the power of who you know. Do not replace what you know by who you know!

I have stopped expecting that my school network should help me, favoring others only because I am in some way connected to them, hiring people because I know them, or expecting favors and returning favors for favors sake.

I have adopted evaluating and selecting people solely based on their skills and talent, using networks to open doors but not more, bringing a sense of impersonal fairness in my dealings and prioritizing honesty above all else.

Should I project a more successful life than I have achieved?

Who do we really live for? Are our actions shaped by what others would see and say? Do we act only to appear smart or educated, popular and successful to others? In too many cultures, appearance is more important than actual facts. This is not only the case with certain Eastern cultures but look at the modern Facebook-driven cultures worldwide. We go to great lengths to create a perception of who we are to gain acceptance and approval from those around us. But, how genuine is this? Are we living our lives in a state of denial and who loses most in this case?

I have stopped thinking that my house, my car, and my job define me, spending endless time and energy on my appearance, worrying about what others may or may not think (in most cases they really do not care anyway) and competing on outward symbols like overt displays of wealth.

I have adopted a belief that a façade hurts me more than anybody else, understanding that my mind, my talent, and my effort define me, influencing others positively and competing only on substantive matters.

How much risk should I embrace?

Human beings face a great paradox: on the one hand, we desire to settle down, to secure our position and to minimize our risks; and on the other hand, we desire adventure, to seek a better position and to be thrilled. On the one hand, we want stability, predictability, and security. On the other hand, we desire new experiences, excitement and growth. A successful person is one who can balance both these traits. We need a good dose of stability while encouraging a fair share of risk-taking. The statistician-philosopher Nassim

Taleb calls this the Barbell Strategy—maximizing reward by balancing the extremes of risk (little risk and a lot risk).

I have stopped seeking life-time jobs, cherishing consistency, advocating for conformity, seeing the world as black or white, or minimizing all risks.

I have adopted seeking improving careers, cherishing change, championing difference, seeing the world as a rainbow of colors, and embracing risks wisely.

Should I always trust my teachers?

What is a better way to encourage a child's creativity: teach her an encyclopedia of knowledge that she should not question or make her question a single theorem? Traditionally, education is inculcated to a child in an almost factory-like process. Set curriculums, set books, and set subjects are taught to children without giving them an opportunity to challenge what they are being taught. In many parts of the world, the education system follows a Church or Missionary-inspired format where knowledge is considered sacred and questioning such knowledge is a sin. Unfortunately, in today's modern and complex world this approach is guaranteed to create unproductive children ill-equipped to deal with the fast-changing environment around them.

We can only get to the bottom of a problem by asking why. Sakachi Toyoda, "King of Japanese Inventors," father of the Japanese Industrialization and founder of Toyota Industries, Co. Ltd. came up with the Five-Whys technique—when faced with any problem, ask why five times in succession to get to the root cause of the problem.

I have stopped believing that teachers/ masters/ elders should never be questioned, taking things for granted and assuming that it is rude to ask questions of an expert, focusing on short-term goals, rushing to judgments, accelerating decisions, or developing speedy and narrow solutions for big problems.

I have adopted a habit of always challenging the norm, taking things with a grain of salt and encouraging teaching using the Socratic method, whereby teachers teach by repeatedly asking questions, practices ensuring that I have an open mind, weighing short-term and long-term pros and cons in all that I do, sleeping over difficult decisions, and setting time aside daily for meditation and reflection.

Bias is our greatest weakness

Throughout history, great leaders have shared one common attribute: the ability to self-reflect. In other words, great leaders are characterized by their ability to set time aside, abstract from the daily routine of life, and ponder deeply on where they are going in life. Another word for self-reflection is self-awareness. Peter Drucker calls it feedback analysis. You will be surprised as to how wrong we often are about ourselves. We are naturally biased to over-compensate when we consider our own abilities and under-compensate when we consider others abilities. Only taking time aside to think carefully about our decisions and about life can correct such biases.

This is especially important when we think about our customers and business partners. Our own biases are often hard to catch, but are usually based on stereotypes that are inaccurate. We should always allow room in our minds to come to a thorough and real understanding of those with whom we are dealing before we make decisions about them.

I am equally at home in America and Asia Pacific. I have spent my adult life and have raised my family in the United States. But there are times where I am still treated like an outsider.

I was once in a high-end men's clothing store in Washington state and as I glanced through the racks of designer sports coats and silk dress shirts, I soon noticed a salesperson follow closely behind me and fix each item immediately after I touched it. I became so frustrated and insulted, I left the store.

Perhaps it is part of human nature to mistrust others that look different from us, and to assume people with a certain appearance think in a particular way. But it is a part of our nature that will cause us to make mistakes every time.

Does that person have a different skin color? An accent? Is their brand of clothing or choice of hairstyle outside of our frame of reference? How do we know if someone is really similar or different than we are? And does that even impact what types of products or services they will choose? Does everyone with the same appearance make the same choice? No. Do people that look similar to us always want what we want? No. Then perhaps should we shouldn't be surprised that we don't fully understand those that look different from us as well.

It is important that entrepreneurs and leaders pay very careful attention when they design their products, market their offerings, and interact with their customers that they do not fall into preconceived models of who their customers ought to look like.

Unfortunately, experiences like mine are common. Some may even shock you.

The car dealer

Rich Beem won the 2002 PGA Championship at Hazeltine National, one of golf's four major tournaments. He shot a par seventy-two in the first round, but followed that with a six-under-sixty-six in the second round to pull into a five-way tie for first place. In the third round, he again shot seventy-two and found himself alone in second place, three strokes behind leader Justin Leonard. In the fourth round, Beem fended off all-American star Tiger Woods, who birdied his last four holes but finished one shot behind Beem, who shot a final round sixty-eight to Woods' sixty-nine. That victory put Beem, who was little-known back then, on the map and helped establish the athlete in the top twenty of the Official World Golf Ranking. Before Beem became the undisputed champion of the most white-collar of sports, he used to earn seven dollars an hour selling car stereos and cell-phones in Seattle. Beem is another poster boy for an American rags-to-riches story.

After his 2002 PGA win, Beem wanted to splurge on something he had always longed for—a luxury car. The Monday after the tournament, Beem and his wife visited a car dealership with the intent to fulfill that longstanding dream.

True to his humble roots, Beem was not dressed in an expensive Armani suit, nor did he strut around parading his medal and all the newspaper and magazine clippings with his picture-making headlines. He wore his regular clothes and talked his regular talk. As such, nobody recognized him at the dealership. The car salesman ignored Beem, treated him indifferently, and wrote him off without even talking to him!

"Nobody wanted to help me because I was wearing shorts, sneakers, and a baseball cap," Beem later said, smiling. "Nobody recognized me. My wife said I could buy whatever I felt like. Personally, I didn't like the salesman very much. When you deal in high-end cars, most of your clientele comes in dressed in suits. You get a guy coming in with shorts and beat-up sneakers and a baseball cap, you're pretty sure he's not going to buy anything."

The dealership not only lost one customer that day because they judged Beem by the way he was dressed and looked, but they lost a marketing opportunity that would have endeared them to their clientele. There are very few more desired patronages for a luxury car dealership than a PGA champion advocating for your product and your service. What a loss!

Trois Pommes boutique

In 2013, the popular American media host, Oprah Winfrey, experienced what she termed a "racist" exchange at the posh, high-end Trois Pommes store in Zurich. Ms. Winfrey's accolades could fill a book: she is Chairwoman and CEO of Chicago-based Harpo Studios, she is Chairwoman and CEO of the Oprah Winfrey Network, she is a very popular and well-read author, she is an award-winning actor, she was awarded the Presidential Medal of Freedom by President Barack Obama, she has an honorary doctorate degree from Harvard, and she is the first African American woman billionaire. In fact, Ms. Winfrey is so popular, especially among young and middle-aged American women, that she can turn a product into an overnight success simply by showcasing that product on her show. In the business circles, the "Oprah Effect" is a measurable impact created by an endorsement from Ms. Winfrey that can suddenly turn a small, unprofitable business into a multi-million dollar company. In short, Ms. Winfrey's picture is the image you would pay millions of dollars to have on your product marketing brochures.

Ms. Winfrey made the trip to Switzerland to attend the wedding of another very popular African American woman, the artist and singer, Ms. Tina Turner. While there, she strolled around Zurich and stopped by the chic Trois Pommes boutique. On display behind a glass case was a $38,000 Tom Ford bag. The "Jennifer" bag was named after actress Jennifer Aniston, who appeared on Ms. Winfrey's TV show and holds Ms. Winfrey in high regards. Ms. Winfrey asked the store clerk if she could take a look at the bag. The clerk's answer stunned her!

The clerk said, "No, it's too expensive. No, no, no you want to see this one because that one will cost too much. You won't be able to afford that one. I don't want to hurt your feelings." Ms. Winfrey replied, "Okay, thank you so much, you're probably right I can't afford it."

Black turtlenecks

Steve Jobs was the world's most iconic CEO for many reasons. One was the fact that he always wore blue jeans, sneakers, and a black turtleneck. This is hardly the outfit of a kingmaker. Compared to the buttoned down suits of Wall Street bankers and Midwestern executives, Mr. Jobs' clothes were at best plain and bland.

In his autobiography, he explained that he got the idea of a simple dress code when he visited a Sony factory in the early 1980s. Noticing that Sony workers wore uniforms, Mr. Jobs asked Sony chairman Akio Morita for the reason. Mr. Morita explained that after the war, "no one had any clothes and companies like Sony had to give their workers something to wear each day." Jobs' auto-biographer, Walter Issaacson, further explained, "over the years, the uniforms developed into their own signature styles and it became a way of bonding workers to the company."

Mr. Jobs liked the idea of a simple dress code that creates such strong bond so much that he asked the famous designer Issey Miyake to create a uniform for Apple workers. However, nobody at Apple wanted to be told how to dress. So Mr. Jobs turned the idea into his personal uniform. He felt that having a known set of clothes to wear is convenient and convey a unique signature style. Since then, countless Silicon Valley CEOs, entrepreneurs, and aspiring leaders have copied Mr. Jobs. They dress simple not because they cannot afford better clothes, but because it brings out their individualism.

L'habit ne fait pas le moine*

* French proverb "The clothes do not a monk make" or "Do not judge a book by its cover"

Can we really tell if a someone is likely to buy a product simply based on their clothing, age, or some other aspect of their appearance? Is our perspective more limited than we realize? In the modern day and age, it is not only insulting and off the mark to judge a person by their outward appearance, it is a business sin! As the many examples in this chapter show, sometimes those who we believe are the antithesis of our customer profile are in fact the epitome of our much desired customer base.

The customer generation in this post-modern, high technology world is very different than the previous, hierarchical-minded generation. The most successful persons today often times do not want to be flashy, do not want to be artificial, and do not necessarily want to seek the opinions and acceptance of others. They put prime importance on personal identity. They value creativity, independence, and inventiveness. They shun conformance, standards, and compliance. Accordingly, your modern customer will not fit a preconceived mold or model from the last generation. They will not look like you or those who you associate with, yet they are very much those who you need for your business to thrive.

It is not sound business to base your sales decision on such non-market factors. Business judgment should be based on a customer's willingness to pay (WTP) and not his or her appearance on whether she is able to pay. No economic theory can be right by assuming an external outlook of the customers.

Now, it is easier said than done to avoid the traps discussed in this chapter. It requires persistent initiatives from leaders to ensure that their companies, their products, and their staff do not get swayed by how they perceive their customers. It takes courage to put aside biases and prejudices that may have been instituted in our environment or learnt since childhood. Even large companies many times fall into these traps. Former First Lady Michelle Obama recounted her experience when once she went incognito to a Target store in the Washington areas as follows: "The only person who came up to me in the store was a woman who asked me to help her take something off a shelf," Mrs. Obama said. "Because she didn't see me as the first lady, she saw me as someone who could help her."

Our habits are acquired behavior patterns that we regularly follow until it has become almost involuntary. Such a trait can be either tremendously advantageous or tremendously disadvantageous. When we adopt a good habit, we do not need to spend energy benefitting from such a habit—it comes naturally to us. On the other hand, a bad habit can be very hard to shake off and can have disastrous consequences, especially when it impacts others around us. Since every business interaction is a human interaction, a good habit that makes others comfortable around us can win deals, and inversely a bad habit that frustrates others can cost us deals.

CHAPTER 11

HOW DO I LIGHT MY FIRE?

"We are what we repeatedly do. Excellence then, is not an act, but a habit."
ARISTOTLE

"Wherever you go, go with all your heart."
CONFUCIUS

"Order and simplification are the first steps towards the mastery of a subject."
THOMAS MANN

"You have to fight to reach your dream. You have to sacrifice and work hard for it."
LIONEL MESSI, FOOTBALLER AND CHAMPION

I WAS BORN IN THE CITY OF DAEGU in post-war Korea. Today, South Korea is one of the powerhouses of the modern world. Often considered the Germany of Asia, it is a nation churning $1.5 trillion in nominal GDP making the country the eleventh largest market economy in the world. The country is home to multinational conglomerates like Samsung and LG in the Consumer Electronics market and Hyundai and Kia in the Automotive market. The nation not only enjoys a high standard of living and modernization but also has seen major booms in industrialization, technological advancement, educational development, and urbanization. The world witnessed how much the Korean nation had transformed itself over the past decades, a transformation often dubbed "the Miracle of the Han river," when the country hosted the Summer Olympics in 1988 and the FIFA World Cup in 2002. But, while today South Korea is rich enough to send aid to several poor countries, it was not always so.

When I was born, South Korea was a very different place. Like most societies that experience the savagery and inexplicable destruction of war, South Korea emerged from the internecine conflict in 1953 with scars that were not easily healed. Those who survived the Korean Wars could hardly be called lucky. Before the war, they lived under Japanese occupation for thirty-six years. Then during World War II they became an accessory in the fight between the Allies and the Axis. And, soon after World War II they lived through the tragedies leading to and during the Korean War. All along, the Korean people suffered greatly, lacking food and sanitation. Diseases, repression, torture, and even mass killings were rampant.

By the time I was born, the Korean people were simply trying to piece their lives together. It was already hard to make sense of the horrors of the recent decades. The psychological wounds were still very fresh. It was as if a whole generation had lived their lives not ever knowing the joy that comes with optimism and hope. But, it was also a generation that was not ready to give up. Somehow these Korean survivors found the willpower to forge ahead. Maybe that fortitude came from their deep conservative tradition, or maybe from their sense of family and social duty or maybe they saw in the eyes of their children the hope of prosperity, which they themselves could not experience. My father was the embodiment of that generation.

I was close to my father. He was more than a father figure to me. In the midst of this grim environment, he was the pillar that stood tall, the rock that could not be broken, the fixture that not only provided safety, protection, and comfort but that also provided meaning to me. As long as he was around, I did not have to think too hard about life. I did not have to resolve the many conflicting signals and emotions in my surroundings. I only had to look up to my father, and like a compass, he would guide me. And, I knew that his guidance would be right. I effectively outsourced all thinking and all planning to my father. Sigmund Freud was reported to have said, "I cannot think of any need in childhood as strong as the need for a father's protection." In my case, my father fulfilled that need in all the spheres of my life. But then, one day in my teenage years, my father suddenly passed away.

Like a sinkhole that appears one day in your backyard, I felt this huge gap coming into my life in a manner that I was never prepared for nor expecting. What was worse, I fell into that sink-hole and went into deep depression. I could not concentrate on anything. I could not wrap my head around what was happening to me. My family and friends could not soothe me. I could not make sense of anything else anymore.

I quit school and sought refuge in the beautiful mountains surrounding Daegu. Like a hermit or a Buddhist monk, for six continuous months I would wake up every morning and make my way up the hills. I would rarely carry food or water with me. I would take a trail that was not often frequented and trekked to a high spot from where I would have an unobstructed view of the surrounding hills, the scattered hamlets in the valley, and the Daegu Air Force Base. That base was instrumental in the Korean War and at the time was being used by the US Air Force. From my vantage point far away, I could see the entire hubbub on the airstrip. With loud roars, fighter jets would speed down the runways and take flight like majestic eagles soaring in the air. They would swerve, bank, maneuver, and disappear in the clouds or over the horizon. Other planes would approach, as if coming back home tired after a long journey and land to go rest in the hangars.

This constant going and coming mesmerized me. There is something to planes that is almost mystic. Maybe it is the fact that they can fly, something we humans could never physically achieve. Maybe, it is the fact that they go to faraway places that most of us cannot go. Or maybe, it is the fact that they are evidences of man's ingenuity at conquering even the far reaches of our Earth. As a boy, I would simply sit and gaze at these airplanes. I have always looked at nature and things around me, and my mind wanders.

I am more than curious. I wonder and marvel at little details. I would question and try to uncover meanings. I would search for Blake's "world in a grain of sand / and a heaven in a wild flower." So, there on the mountains of Daegu, I would sit in the grass and among the trees, left by myself and accompanied only by the soft whistling of the wind and the chirping of the birds, from morning till dusk, and ponder. And, I started to feel that spark in me.

On the mountains of Daegu, as I gazed at these metal birds subjecting the surroundings to their control, I started to believe again in the capabilities of man, in the goodness of life, and in the hope of a yet uncharted future. I started to realize that man could innovate, could build, could drive, could fly, could soar, and could come back home safely to comfort and rest. I started to dream of worlds beyond the clouds pierced by the airplanes, of lands afar, of realms unimagined. I felt the spark glowing inside me and its warmth filling me. My depression gradually gave way to confidence. My grimness slowly gave way to hope. I was being transformed in a way that would forever change my life. The wars from the past would be surmounted; the sadness of the present would not shackle me anymore; only the promise of the future mattered. At the end of these six months of virtual self-exile on the mountains of Daegu, gazing at the airplanes, my fire was lit. I knew exactly where I needed to go and nothing could or would be able to stop me. As a fatherless child in a poor family living in a post-war and struggling country, the only country that my family members and my neighbors had ever known, I made up my mind—I would go to the United States of America and make it big there!

Over the next several years, I would work diligently in Korea as a young man with this fire burning in me, pushing me, encouraging me, and inspiring me. I made my way through my personal life and my professional career with renewed vigor. At every step, I would work very hard to achieve my dream. I would fall but then would get up standing taller. I would fail but then would try harder. I never looked back. It took me two full decades before finally landing in Los Angeles. Throughout, the fire that was lit on the mountains of Daegu never abated.

Driving force

What is it that pushes us to get up every morning and go about our lives? Where does our energy to face daily challenges come from? And why is it that some of us go farther than others, work harder than others, fight stronger than others, and win bigger than others? Why is it that some of us are never satisfied and never cease improving our lot? Conversely, why is it that some of us are happy with the status quo, give up easily, and accept mediocre outcomes?

At the core of everything we do is the reason to do it. Let us explore this thinking and peel away the layers of why we do what we do. Let us ask ourselves the question of why we put ourselves through the daily pains to get up, go and work, whether be it in an office or in a shop or on the street, rather than sit back and enjoy a leisurely life of doing nothing. The easy and immediate answer is we go to work to earn money. That is a logical and an economic reason. But, why do we need money? We earn money so that we can buy the things we need to lead a decent life. Now, that is a personal and perhaps a survival reason.

Okay, why then do we need a decent life? We want to lead a decent life so that our kids, our families, and we do not suffer from the lack of life's basic necessities. Now, that is a social and perhaps an evolutionary reason. Fair enough. But, then why is it that we work very hard to earn much more than the minimum required to ensure the survival of our genes? What is it that is unique in the human species that drives us to achieve tremendous outcomes? What pushes us to create value beyond the normal? Why is growth so important to all businesses? Is there a single rational reason for putting ourselves through all the travails of a man-made life to achieve larger-than-life successes?

Beyond reason, there is a fire that burns in our hearts. There is a desire to achieve more than our physical limits. There is an aspiration to push us further. There is a hunger to not just win, but to win big. There is a craving to go where we have not been before. There is an appetite that is only satiated with new experiences. There is a fascination with the unknown. There is an ambition for super achievements. There is a yearning in our soul for greatness!

Some believe that this fire is not present in all of us. Others believe that we are born with a fire but the intensity is fixed in us. Hence, some of us push hard, some harder, and others not at all. William Shakespeare wrote, "Some are born great, some achieve greatness, and some have greatness thrust upon them."

My personal take, based on my life-long experience, is we are all born with the spark for greatness and it is up to us to light this spark into a warm and illuminating fire or extinguish it into cold gray ash. And the first step to light up this fire in one's heart is to realize it is there and to convince oneself that it can be lit up like a torch.

It is important for each one of us to seek to light the fire in our hearts. The process to do so is personal. There is no written script. There is no manual. There is no quick solution. Instead, you need to be truthful and genuine to yourself. You need to convince yourself first that you have in you the means to achieve greatness. You have to remove the shackles that tie down your mindsets. You need to let aspirations drive your will. You need to believe that man's ability to achieve is boundless. And you need to believe that you, despite where you have been before or where life has placed you today, that you can achieve it all. And, once you have done that, there is absolutely nothing that can stop you.

Liang and the online art store

I met Liang on a cold winter day in October 2014 in Singapore. Professor Wong Poh Kam, who runs the Entrepreneurship Center at the National University of Singapore, had invited me to come and speak to the EMBA class as a guest speaker. The NUS MBA program, under the leadership of Dean Bernard Yeung, stands among the best-ranked business school programs in the world and attracts very bright students from across Asia and elsewhere. After my speech, I asked the students from the Entrepreneurship Club to give me a one-minute pitch on ideas they have been musing upon and trying to turn into start-up businesses while they are still in college.

Liang was vice president of the club and I remembered him as a shy boy who stepped up to introduce his start-up concept as China's first dedicated online store connecting artists with art enthusiasts. Liang immediately impacted me as being different from the other young adults who presented before him. His passion for his idea radiated from his face. His eyes lit up as soon as he took the stage. His voice was clear and I could feel the excitement in his words. His whole body suddenly became active when he started talking about the concept. I knew within the first few seconds after Liang stood up and started to speak that this kid had found the fire burning in his heart, just like I had found my fire on the mountains of Daegu a long time ago. Seeing the passion in Liang transported me to that time when I discovered my own passion. He had, in fact, discovered a passion before discovering a business model. Before he even started presenting his business plan, I knew that Liang would be successful at what he wants to do. At that precise moment, in an almost metaphysical or karmic way, I saw myself in Liang.

Liang had the idea of creating an online store and forum to connect young Chinese consumers with Western art. He had detected a trend among the youth in China who were being exposed to Western culture and had been quickly developing an appreciation for Western art. Liang envisioned an online portal where these young adults would come to learn about art and order high quality giclee prints of their favorite Van Gogh or Matisse. He also believed that this consumer base would be interested in vintage posters, works from famous photographers, and high quality prints of their own personal pictures. In short, Liang was thinking about creating a Chinese Art.Com.

After his brief presentation, Liang approached me and asked if I would be his mentor. I felt he was doing me a favor asking me to help realize his dreams. Over the next several months, I spent time with Liang in person whenever I was in Singapore or via Skype and phone when elsewhere to review his concepts. The first thing I worked on with Liang was to retool the business plans by placing the customer at the center of it all. We reimagined the complete idea with serving the customer needs. We explored in-depth the intended customer base. While we concluded that the youth indeed have interest in art, they also have limited income. We identified the older Chinese neo-rich as a potential adjacent segment. We studied where these consumer segments were learning about art. We looked at what information they were seeking, whether the information was satisfying their curiosity or not, and whether the information was accurate. We studied the competition, which consisted of large online stores like Taobao with a section selling artwork. Within a short time, we realized that there is a very viable and growing customer segment for the type of products Liang has in mind. Liang's initial objective of reaching $1 million in sales in five years was clearly a goal that could be beat many times over.

With this customer approach, I coached Liang to position all his decisions with customer experience always in mind. Liang deprioritized the Web site technology and on my advice started looking at outsourcing the whole Web design. Instead, I asked that he focus on identifying, meeting, and exceeding the needs of his planned customer base. The language for coding the Web site did not matter; what mattered was whether the customer felt attracted to the Web site design. This being a Web site selling art, it had to display artistic beauty.

In the weeks that followed, Liang explored a whole new business model. He reached out to a dozen artists in Dafen Village in Shenzhen. Artists there are famous for mass production of art replicas. I encouraged Liang to work the logistics where he could take orders online, have these artists make replicas within twenty-four hours and then ship the replicas out the following day. Having built enough confidence, I challenged Liang to shoot for a $10 million revenue goal within three years! Now equipped with a bold vision, young Liang's passion turned into dedicated enthusiasm that he put to work for several hours daily. He refined his business plans, established contacts, built a network, researched equipment, analyzed costs, and grew his own knowledge of art.

By June 2015, I felt Liang's fledgling business had been solidly refined with a strong customer experience focus. He was now ready for the big surprise I had for him. I called Liang up and asked him to be ready to make a trip to Shanghai. I wanted Liang to meet an old friend of mine, Yun, who has been running an online store in China for several years now. Yun is a successful and serial entrepreneur in his own right. He had started an eCommerce site, known as mySimon, which he later sold to CNET for several hundreds of million dollars. Over the past twenty years, we maintained a close relationship. During that time, Yun started and exited four separate companies previously and was onto his latest idea. He is the definite expert in the Chinese online marketplace whom I always call upon.

Liang was going to have an M&A discussion with Yun at a time when he only had a business plan, a draft Web site, and unbridled enthusiasm. Liang arrived at Yun's office in Shanghai fifteen minutes early. The night before I had given him a crash course in business negotiation. Liang and Yun connected easily. They both felt each other's energy. And, Yun was immediately sold on the online art store idea. He saw the value of the proposal from the end customer point of view and he realized the market potential. Yun made an offer to incorporate Liang's business plan into his company… at a multi-million dollar valuation! Yun further made yet another important decision—he hired Liang to run the business within his own company. He too saw the fire burning in Liang's heart and knew that Liang would move heaven and earth to get the business to succeed. He was, of course, both wise and correct in doing so!

Why did I share this story about Liang? He is not a sixty-year old CEO of a large Fortune 50 company. No, Liang was a shy MBA student in Singapore with an idea that he was passionate about. He redirected his business plan away from all noise, like which Web technology to use, to focus on customer experience. Along the way, he discovered new customer segments, new products, new channels to serve the customer, and new revenue models. Successful businesses are always built around the customer. Liang also had the most important ingredient for success—he was deeply passionate about what he wanted to do. In fact, I believe this is beyond passion—he discovered the fire that burns inside him. This fire would not let him fail, would push him constantly, would make him work hard, would carry him the extra mile and would keep him in a positive, constructive mood all along. Liang had many things going on in his life—he was a student away from home with expectations from his parents and from his school. But these did not deter him from pursuing his dream. He made it all work despite the pressure and many challenges along the way.

I believe that Liang listened to and adopted the many lessons I covered in this book. He was willing to think deeply and wonder why and what and how. He sought out mentorship and he was willing to adapt his business plan while never letting go of his fire. These are perspectives and habits that have helped me to achieve success and that I believed would make Liang successful too.

After reading this book, I hope you will keep these two factors in mind whenever you are designing, implementing, and running your businesses: internally, *light your fire* and externally, *focus on the customer.* If you can wonder deeply about what motivates you, what drives you, and you can wonder deeply about what drives your customers, nothing will stop you from succeeding in your business. Be firmly rooted in what you want to do. If you are not convinced that this is what you desire for yourself and your family, then try to move out and do something else. You cannot achieve tremendous success in a field that you are not passionate about. You will never give it your 110 percent. Once you have that, give total attention to meeting your customer needs. Make every decision, asking yourself whether the decision will improve your position vis-à-vis your customer. If you face a setback, ask questions until you find the key to your customers' needs.

My friends often give me the title of CCO—Chief Criticism Officer! We must continually ask questions that dig deep. We must look critically at ourselves, our company's, our customers, to stay relevant and meet the needs and capture the imagination of a changing world. As soon as we cease wondering we will begin the process of decline. I hope you will have your own journey of always wondering. Farewell!

Made in the USA
Middletown, DE
03 December 2017